AF568144

SCIENCE OF GRAMINOIDS

SCIENCE OF GRAMINOIDS

By

Dr. H. Shivanna

Professor & Head

Deptt. of Forest Biology & Tree Improvement

College of Forestry, SIRSI

Uttar Kannada

Karnataka (India)

DISCOVERY PUBLISHING HOUSE PVT. LTD.

NEW DELHI-110 002

Published by:

Tilak Wasan

DISCOVERY PUBLISHING HOUSE PVT. LTD.
4383/4B, Ansari Road, Darya Ganj
New Delhi-110 002 (India)
Phone : +91-11-23279245, 43596064-65
Fax : +91-11-23253475
E-mail : parul.wasan@gmail.com
discoverypublishinghouse@gmail.com
web : www.discoverypublishinggroup.com

***First Edition:* 2013**

ISBN: 978-93-5056-298-7

Science of Graminoids

Printed at:
Dynamic Printers
Delhi

Preface

Grasses, or more technically graminoids, are monocotyledonous, usually herbaceous plants with narrow leaves growing from the base. They include the 'true grasses', of the Poaceae (or Gramineae) family, as well as the sedges (Cyperaceae) and the rushes (Juncaceae). The true grasses include cereals, bamboo and the grasses of lawns (turf) and grassland. Sedges include many wild marsh and grassland plants, and some cultivated ones such as water chestnut (*Eleocharis dulcis*) and papyrus sedge (*Cyperus papyrus*). Uses for graminoids include food (as grain, sprouted grain, shoots or rhizomes), drink (beer, whisky), pasture for livestock, thatch, paper, fuel, clothing, insulation, construction, sports turf, basket weaving and many others.

Graminoids are among the most versatile life forms. They became widespread toward the end of the Cretaceous period, and fossilized dinosaur dung (coprolites) have been found containing phytoliths of a variety of grasses that include grasses that are related to modern rice and bamboo. Grasses have adapted to conditions in lush rain forests, dry deserts, cold mountains and even intertidal habitats, and are now the most widespread plant type; grass is a valuable source of food and Energy for all sorts of wildlife and organics.

Graminoids are the dominant vegetation in many habitats, including grassland, salt-marsh, reedswamp and steppes. They also occur as a smaller part of the vegetation in almost every other terrestrial habitat.

Grasses are the main plant species in verges along roads, railways and on river dikes. It is difficult to get an idea how many hectares are involved in this type of land cover. Along highways, main and small roads, along railways and rivers, strips of some metres of width all over hundreds of kilometres are overgrown with grass, herbs, shrubs and trees. One may count some 3000 m^2 of verges per running km, giving an enormous capacity for carbon sequestration, mostly for a long period of time. Besides the presence of grass species in fallow terrains are also an enormous carbon sink, although in these sites the situation lasts for a long period so that balance does not change.

In the frame of the EU Directive 2078/92 "Farming practices compatible with the requirements of protection of the environment and natural resources, as well as maintenance of the countryside and the landscape", the member states may conclude agreements with farmers for sowing grass or another cover crop after a main crop (cereals, maize) to prevent the leaching of nitrates and minerals and to prevent wind and water erosion during winter time. In Flanders, the Government contracted 4.240 farmers with about 50.000 hectares for this arrangement in 2006. Under the same Directive, the authorities can make a long term agreement (5-10 years) with farmers for the management of buffer zones (5 m width) between arable land along small streams or a wood for an increasing biodiversity. In Flanders, it means a total area of 1.600 ha under this management system.

In more modern times (1950s) the sugar industry used vetiver grass quite widely as contour conservation hedges and for the stabilization of road sides and embankments. Vetiver once thought to be confined to wetlands thrives over a range of ecological conditions.

In cases, set-aside and riparian buffer zones and woods, concern arable land converted to grassland. But this is only a small fraction of the grassland area lost in Europe during the last decades.

It is clear that these types of grasslands respond very much to the new EU policy for maintaining and enlarging the biodiversity, animal welfare, development of the countryside, etc., directed in the respective regulations and directives.

—Author

Contents

CHAPTER – 1

Introduction

Grasses, or more technically graminoids, are monocotyledonous, usually herbaceous plants with narrow leaves growing from the base. They include the 'true grasses', of the Poaceae (or Gramineae) family, as well as the sedges (Cyperaceae) and the rushes (Juncaceae). The true grasses include cereals, bamboo and the grasses of lawns (turf) and grassland. Sedges include many wild marsh and grassland plants, and some cultivated ones such as water chestnut (*Eleocharis dulcis*) and papyrus sedge (*Cyperus papyrus*). Uses for graminoids include food (as grain, sprouted grain, shoots or rhizomes), drink (beer, whisky), pasture for livestock, thatch, paper, fuel, clothing, insulation, construction, sports turf, basket weaving and many others.

Graminoids are among the most versatile life forms. They became widespread toward the end of the Cretaceous period, and fossilized dinosaur dung (coprolites) have been found containing phytoliths of a variety of grasses that include grasses that are related to modern rice and bamboo. Grasses have adapted to conditions in lush rain forests, dry deserts, cold mountains and even intertidal habitats, and are now the most widespread plant type; grass is a valuable source of food and energy for all sorts of wildlife and organics.

Graminoids are the dominant vegetation in many habitats, including grassland, salt-marsh, reedswamp and steppes. They also occur as a smaller part of the vegetation in almost every other terrestrial habitat.

There are some 3,500 species of graminoids.

Many types of animals eat grass as their main source of food, and are called *graminivores* — these include cattle, sheep, horses, rabbits and many invertebrates, such as grasshoppers and the caterpillars of many brown butterflies. Grasses are also eaten by omnivorous or even occasionally by primarily carnivorous animals.

In the study of ecological communities, herbaceous plants are divided into graminoids and *forbs*, which are herbaceous dicotyledons, mostly with broad leaves.

Plants of this type have always been important to humans. They have been grown as food for domesticated animals for up to 6,000 years. They have been used for paper-making since 2400 BC or before. Now they provide the majority of food crops, and have many other uses, such as feeding animals, and for lawns. There are many minor uses, and grasses are familiar to most human cultures.

Lawns

In some places, particularly in suburban areas throughout the world, the maintenance of a grass lawn is a sign of a homeowner's responsibility to the overall appearance of their neighbourhood. One work credits lawn maintenance to "...the desire for upward mobility and its manifestation in the lawn. As Virginia Jenkins, author of *The Lawn*, put it quite bluntly, 'Upper middle-class Americans emulated aristocratic society with their own small, semi-rural estates.' In general, the lawn was one of the primary selling points of these new suburban homes, as it shifted social class designations from the equity and ubiquity of urban homes connected to the streets with the upper-middle class designation of a 'healthy' green space and the status symbol that is the front lawn".

Many municipalities and homeowner's associations have rules which require lawns to be maintained to certain specifications, sanctioning those who allow the grass to grow too long. In communities with drought problems, watering of lawns may be restricted to certain times of day or days of the week.

The smell of the freshly cut grass is produced mainly by cis-3-Hexenal.

Sports Turf

Grass is important in many sports, notably with those played on fields such as American football, Association football, baseball, cricket, and rugby. In some sports facilities, including indoor domes and places where maintenance of a grass field would be difficult, grass may be replaced with artificial turf, a synthetic grass-like substitute. Sports such as golf, tennis and cricket are particularly dependent on the quality of the grass on which the sport is played.

Cricket

In cricket, the pitch is the strip of carefully mowed and rolled grass where the bowler bowls. In the days leading up to the match it is repeatedly mowed and rolled to produce a very hard, flat surface for the ball to bounce off. The quality of the preparation can have a considerable influence on the game; a relatively grassy pitch will favour bowlers and a hard and dryer pitch, with less grass remaining, will typically favour batsmen (at least initially). As the grass dries out and is damaged over the course of the match the pitch's characteristics will change, resulting in batting on the first day of a test match being vastly different to batting on the same pitch after 7 days of play.

Golf

Golf is very dependent on a quality grass surface. Grass on golf courses is kept in three distinct conditions: that of the *rough*, the *fairway*, and the *putting green*. Grass on the fairway is short and even, allowing the player to cleanly strike the ball. Playing from the rough is a disadvantage because the grass is generally much longer, which may affect the flight of the ball. Grass on the putting green is the shortest and most even, ideally allowing the ball to roll smoothly over the surface. An entire industry revolves around the development and marketing of grasses for golf courses.

Tennis

In tennis, grass is grown on very hard-packed soil, and the bounce of a tennis-ball may vary depending on the grass's health, how recently it has been mowed, and the wear and tear of recent play. The surface is softer than hard courts and clay (other tennis surfaces), so the ball bounces lower, and players must reach the ball faster resulting in a different style of play which may suit some players more than others. The most famous grass tennis court in the world is Centre Court at Wimbledon located in England, home of the Wimbledon Championship. This is considered the most expensive lawn in the world.

Fiction

Grass plays a central role in two important science fiction catastrophe novels from the 1940s and 1950s, Ward Moore's *Greener Than You Think*, in which the world is slowly taken over by unstoppable Bermuda Grass, and John Christopher's *The Death of Grass*, in which a plague that kills off all forms of grass threatens the survival of the human species.

CHAPTER – 2

Grassland

Grasslands are areas where the vegetation is dominated by grasses (Poaceae) and other herbaceous (non-woody) plants (forbs). However, sedge (Cyperaceae) and rush (Juncaceae) families can also be found. Grasslands occur naturally on all continents except Antarctica. In temperate latitudes, such as northwestern Europe and the Great Plains and California in North America, native grasslands are dominated by perennial bunch grass species, whereas in warmer climates annual species form a greater component of the vegetation.

Grasslands are found in most ecological regions of the Earth. For example there are five terrestrial ecoregion classifications (subdivisions) of the temperate grasslands, savannas, and shrublands biome ('ecosystem'), which is one of eight terrestrial ecozones of the Earth's surface.

Grassland vegetation can vary in height from very short, as in chalk where the vegetation may be less than 30 cm (12 in) high, to quite tall, as in the case of North American tallgrass prairie, South American grasslands and African savanna. Woody plants, shrubs or trees, may occur on some grasslands — forming savannas, scrubby and surface of the continent of Africa. While grasslands in general support diverse wildlife, given the lack of hiding places for predators, the African Savanna regions support a much greater diversity in wildlife than do temperate grasslands.

The appearance of mountains in the western United States during the Miocene and Pliocene epochs, a period of some 25 million years, created a continental climate favorable to the evolution of grasslands. Existing forest biomes declined, and grasslands became much more widespread. Following the Pleistocene Ice Ages, grasslands expanded in range in the hotter, drier climates, and began to become the dominant land feature worldwide.

As flowering plants, grasses grow in great concentrations in climates where annual rainfall ranges between 500 and 900 mm (20 and 35 in). The root systems of perennial grasses and forbs form complex mats that hold the soil in place. Mites, insect larvae, nematodes and earthworms inhabit deep soil, which can reach 6 metres (20 ft) underground in undisturbed grasslands on the richest soils of the world. These invertebrates, along with symbiotic fungi, extend the root systems, break apart hard soil, enrich it with urea and other natural fertilizers, trap minerals and water and promote growth. Some types of fungi make the plants more resistant to insect and microbial attacks.

Natural grasslands primarily occur in regions that receive between 250 and 900 mm (9.8 and 35 in) of rain per year, as compared with deserts, which receive less than 250 mm (9.8 in) and tropical rainforests, which receive more than 2,000 mm (79 in) .Anthropogenic grasslands often occur in much higher rainfall zones, as high as 200 cm (79 in) annual rainfall. Grassland can exist naturally in areas with higher rainfall when other factors prevent the growth of forests, such as in serpentine barrens, where minerals in the soil inhibit most plants from growing.

Average daily temperatures range between -20 and 30°C. Temperate grasslands have warm summers and cold winters with rain or some snow.

Grassland Biodiversity and Conservation

Grasslands dominated by unsown wild-plant communities ('unimproved grasslands') can be called either natural or 'semi-natural' habitats. The majority of grasslands in temperate climates are 'semi-natural'. Although their plant communities are natural, their maintenance depends upon anthropogenic activities such as low-intensity farming, which maintains these grasslands through grazing and cutting regimes. These grasslands contain many species of wild plants — grasses, sedges, rushes and herbs — 25 or more speerican prairie grasslands or lowland wildflower meadows in the UK are now rare and their associated wild flora equally threatened. Associated with the wild-plant diversity of the 'unimproved' grasslands is usually a rich invertebrate fauna; also there are many species of birds that are grassland 'specialists', such as the snipe and the Great Bustard. Agriculturally improved grasslands, which dominate modern intensive agricultural landscapes, are usually poor in wild plant species due to the original diversity of plants having been destroyed by cultivation, the original wild-plant communities having been replaced by sown monocultures of cultivated varieties of grasses and clovers, such as Perennial ryegrass and White Clover. In many parts of the world 'unimproved' grasslands are one of the least threatened habitats, and a target for acquisition by wildlife conservation groups or for special grants to landowners who are encouraged to manage them appropriately.

Grasslands are of vital importance for raising livestock for human consumption and for milk and other dairy products.

Grassland vegetation remains dominant in a particular area usually due to grazing, cutting, or natural or manmade fires, all discouraging colonisation by and survival of tree and shrub seedlings. Some of the world's largest expanses of grassland are found in African savanna, and these are maintained by wild herbivores as well as by nomadic pastoralists and their cattle, sheep or goats.

Grasslands may occur naturally or as the result of human activity. Grasslands created and maintained by human activity are called anthropogenic grasslands. Hunting peoples around the world often set regular fires to maintain and extend grasslands, and prevent fire-intolerant trees and shrubs from taking hold. The tallgrass prairies in the American Midwest may have been extended eastward into Illinois, Indiana, and Ohio by human agency. Much grassland in northwest Europe developed after the Neolithic Period, when people gradually cleared the forest to create areas for raising their livestock.

Tropical and Subtropical Grasslands

These grasslands are classified with tropical and subtropical savannas and shrublands as the tropical and subtropical grasslands, savannas, and shrublands biome. Notable tropical and subtropical grasslands include the Llanos grasslands of northern South America.

Temperate Grasslands

Mid-latitude grasslands, including the Prairie and Pacific Grasslands of North America, the Pampas of Argentina, Brazil and Uruguay, calcareous downland, and the steppes of Europe. They are classified with temperate savannas and shrublands as the temperate grasslands, savannas, and shrublands biome. Temperate grasslands are the home to many large herbivores, such as bison, gazelles, zebras, rhinoceroses, and wild horses. Carnivores like lions, wolves and cheetahs and leopards are also found in temperate grasslands. Other animals of this region include: deer, prairie dogs, mice, jack rabbits, skunks, coyotes, snakes, fox, owls, badgers, blackbirds (both Old and New World varieties), grasshoppers, meadowlarks, sparrows, quails, hawks and hyenas.

Flooded Grasslands

Grasslands that are flooded seasonally or year-round, like the Everglades of Florida, the Pantanal of Brazil, Bolivia and Paraguay or the Esteros del Ibera in Argentina.They are classified with flooded savannas as the flooded grasslands and savannas biome and occur mostly in the tropics and subtropics.

Montane Grasslands

High-altitude grasslands located on high mountain ranges around the world, like the Páramo of the Andes Mountains. They are part of the montane grasslands and shrublands biome and also constitute tundra.

Tundra Grasslands

Similar to montane grasslands, polar arctic tundra can have grasses, but high soil moisture means that few tundras are grass-dominated today. However, during the Pleistocene ice ages, a polar grassland known as steppe-tundra occupied large areas of the Northern hemisphere. These are in the tundra biome.

Desert and Xeric Grasslands

Also called desert grasslands, this is composed of sparse grassland ecoregions located in the deserts and xeric shrublands biome.

Fauna

Grassland in all its form supports a vast variety of mammals, reptiles, birds, and insects. Typical large mammals include the Blue Wildebeest, American Bison, Giant Anteater and Przewalski's Horse.

There is evidence for grassland being much the product of animal behaviour and movement; some examples include migratory herds of antelope trampling vegetation and African Bush Elephants eating Acacia saplings before the plant has a chance to grow into a mature tree.

Pampas

The Pampas (from Quechua, meaning 'plain') are the fertile South American lowlands, covering more than 750,000 km^2 (289,577 sq mi), that include the Argentine provinces of Buenos Aires, La Pampa, Santa Fe, Entre Ríos and Córdoba, most of Uruguay, and the southernmost Brazilian State, Rio Grande do Sul. These vast plains are only interrupted by the low Ventana and Tandil hills near Bahía Blanca and Tandil (Argentina), with a height of 1,300 m (4,265 ft) and 500 m (1,640 ft) respectively. The climate is mild, with precipitation of 600 mm (23.6 in) to 1,200 mm (47.2 in), more or less evenly distributed through the year, making the soils appropriate for agriculture. This area is also one of the distinct physiography provinces of the larger Paraná-Paraguay Plain division. These plains contain unique wildlife because of the different terrains around it. Some of this wildlife includes the rhea, the badger, and the prairie chicken.

Vegetation

Frequent wildfires ensure that only small plants such as grasses flourish, and trees are rare. The dominant vegetation types are grassy prairie and grass steppe in which numerous species of the grass genus *Stipa* are particularly conspicuous. 'Pampas Grass' (*Cortaderia selloana*) is an iconic species of the Pampas. Vegetation typically includes perennial grasses and herbs. Different strata of grasses occur because of gradients of water availability.

The World Wildlife Fund divides the Pampa into three distinct ecoregions. The Uruguayan savanna lies east of the Uruguay River, and includes all of Uruguay and the southern portion of Brazil's state of Rio Grande do Sul. The Humid Pampas include eastern Buenos Aires Province, and southern Entre Ríos Province. The Semi-arid Pampas includes western Buenos Aires Province and adjacent portions of Santa Fe, Córdoba, and La Pampa provinces. The Pampas are bounded by the drier Argentine espinal grasslands, which form a semicircle around the north, east, and south of the Humid Pampas.

Winters are cool to mild and summers are very warm and humid. Rainfall is fairly uniform throughout the year but is a little heavier during the summer. Annual rainfall is heaviest near the coast and decreases gradually further inland. Rain during the late spring and summer usually arrives in the form of brief heavy showers and thunderstorms. More general rainfall occurs the remainder of the year as cold fronts and storm systems move through. Although cold spells during the winter often send nighttime temperatures below freezing, snow is quite rare. In most winters, a few light snowfalls occur over inland areas.

Central Argentina boasts a successful agricultural business, with crops grown on the Pampas south and west of Buenos Aires. Much of the area is also used for cattle and more recently to grow vineyards in the Buenos Aires wine region. These farming regions (*i.e.*, modified of disturbed Pampas) are particularly susceptible to flooding during heavy rainfall.

Prairie

Prairies are considered part of the temperate grasslands, savannas, and shrublands biome by ecologists, based on similar temperate climates, moderate rainfall, and grasses, herbs, and shrubs, rather than trees, as the dominant vegetation type. Temperate grassland regions include the Pampas of Argentina, Brazil and Uruguay as well as the steppes of Eurasia.

Lands typically referred to as 'prairie' tend to be in North America. The term encompasses the area referred to as the Interior Lowlands of the United States, Canada and Mexico, which includes all of the Great Plains as well as the wetter, somewhat hillier land to the east. In the U.S., the area is constituted by most or all of the states of North Dakota, South Dakota, Nebraska, Kansas, and Oklahoma, and sizable parts of the states of Montana, Wyoming, Colorado, New Mexico, Texas, Missouri, Iowa, Illinois, Indiana, Wisconsin, and western and southern Minnesota. The Central Valley of California is also a prairie. The Canadian Prairies occupy vast areas of Manitoba, Saskatchewan, and Alberta.

The formation of the North American Prairies started with the upwelling of the Rocky Mountains. The mountains created a rain shadow that killed most of the trees.

Most prairie soil was deposited during the last glacial advance that began about 110,000 years ago. The glaciers expanding southward scraped the soil, picking up material and leveling the terrain. As the glaciers retreated about 10,000 years ago, it deposited this material in the form of till.

Tallgrass Prairie evolved over tens of thousands of years with the disturbances of grazing and fire. Native ungulates such as bison, elk, and white-tailed deer, roamed the expansive, diverse, plentiful grassland before European colonization of the Americas. For 10,000-20,000 years native people used fire annually as a tool to assist in hunting, transportation and safety. Evidence of ignition sources of fire in the tallgrass prairie are overwhelmingly human as opposed to lightning. Humans, and grazing animals, were active participants in the process of prairie formation and the establishment of the diversity of graminoid and forbs species. Fire has the effect on prairies of removing trees, clearing dead plant matter, and changing the availability of certain nutrients in the soil from the ash produced. Fire kills the vascular tissue of trees, but not prairie, as up to 75 per cent (depending on the species) of the total plant biomass is below the soil surface and will re-grow from its deep (up to 6 feet) roots. Without disturbance, trees will encroach on a grassland, cast shade, which suppresses the understory. Prairie and widely spaced Oak trees evolved to coexist in the oak savanna ecosystem.

Fertility

In spite of long recurrent droughts and occasional torrential rains, the grasslands of the Great Plains are not subject to great soil erosion. The deep, interconnected root systems of prairie grasses firmly hold the soil in place and prevent run-off of soil. When a plant dies, the fungi, bacteria and the other slowly eat the roots and leaves, returning nutrients to the soil.

These deep roots also help prairie plants to reach water in even the driest conditions. The grass suffers much less damage from dry conditions than the farm crops that have replaced many former prairies.

Types

The types of prairies in North America are usually split into three groups: wet, mesic, and dry.

Wet

In this type of prairie, the soil is usually very moist most of the growing season, and has poor water drainage. This can possibly contain a bog or fen, since it often has plentiful stagnant water. This type of prairie has the best type of farming soil.

Mesic

Mesic prairies (English pronunciation: have good drainage, but have good soil during the growing season. This type of prairie is the most often converted for agricultural usage, consequently it is one of the more endangered types of prairie.

Dry

Dry Prairie is a prairie which has somewhat wet to very dry soil during the growing season because of good drainage in the soil. Often, this prairie can be found on uplands or slopes.

Farming

The very dense soil plagued the first settlers who were using wooden ploughs, which were more suitable for loose forest soil. On the prairie the plows bounced around and the soil stuck to them. This problem was solved in 1837 by an Illinois blacksmith named John Deere who developed a steel moldboard plow that was stronger and cut the roots, making the fertile soils ready for farming.

The tallgrass prairie has been converted into one of the most intensive crop producing areas in North America. Less than one tenth of one per cent (<0.09%) of the original landcover of the tallgrass prairie biome remains. States formerly with landcover in native tallgrass prairie such as Iowa, Illinois, Minnesota, Wisconsin, Nebraska, and Missouri have became valued for their highly productive soils and are included in the Corn Belt. As an example of this land use intensity, Illinois and Iowa for the United States, rank 49th and 50th out of 50 states in total uncultivated land remaining.

Biofuels

Research, by David Tilman, ecologist at the University of Minnesota, suggests that "biofuels made from high-diversity mixtures of prairie plants can reduce global warming by removing carbon dioxide from the atmosphere. Even when grown on infertile soils, they can provide a substantial portion of global energy needs, and leave fertile land for food production." Unlike corn and soybeans which are major food crops, prairie grasses are not used for human consumption. Prairie grasses can be grown in infertile soil, eliminating the cost of adding nutrients to the soil. Tilman and his colleagues estimate that prairie grass biofuels would yield 51 per cent more energy per acre than ethanol from corn grown on fertile land. Some grasses commonly used are lupine, big bluestem (turkey foot), blazing star, switchgrass, and prairie clover.

Preservation

Only one per cent of tallgrass prairie remains in the U.S. today.

Significant preserved areas of prairie include:

- American Prairie Foundation, Phillips and Blaine Counties, Montana
- Ceresco Prairie Conservancy, Ripon College, Wisconsin

- Clymer Meadow Preserve, Hunt County, Texas
- Cypress Hills Interprovincial Park, Alberta and Saskatchewan
- Grasslands National Park, Saskatchewan
- Hoosier Prairie, Lake County, Indiana
- Jennings Environmental Education Centre, Pennsylvania
- Kissimmee Prairie Preserve State Park, Okeechobee County, Florida
- Konza Prairie, Manhattan, Kansas
- Midewin National Tallgrass Prairie, in Will County, Illinois
- Neal Smith National Wildlife Refuge, Iowa
- Nine-Mile Prairie, Nebraska
- Paynes Prairie Preserve State Park, Alachua County, Florida
- Richard Bong State Recreation Area, in Kenosha County, Wisconsin
- Tallgrass Aspen Parkland, Manitoba and Minnesota
- Tallgrass Prairie National Preserve, Kansas
- Tallgrass Prairie Preserve 32,000 acres (130 km^2), Oklahoma
- University of Wisconsin–Madison Arboretum, University of Wisconsin–Madison, Wisconsin
- Zumwalt Prairie, Wallowa County, Oregon

Virgin Prairies

Virgin prairie refers to prairie land that has never been plowed. Small virgin prairies exist in the American Midwestern states and in Canada. Restored prairie refers to a prairie that has been reseeded after plowing or other disturbance.

Prairie Garden

A *prairie garden* is a garden primarily consisting of plants from a prairie.

Savanna

A savanna, or savannah, is a grassland ecosystem characterized by the trees being sufficiently small or widely spaced so that the canopy does not close. The open canopy allows sufficient light to reach the ground to support an unbroken herbaceous layer consisting primarily of C4 grasses. Some classification systems also recognize a grassland savanna from which trees are absent. This article deals only with savanna under the common definition of a grassy woodland with a significant woody plant component.

It is often believed that savannas feature widely spaced, scattered trees. However, in many savannas, tree densities are higher and trees are more regularly spaced than in forest. Savannas are also characterized by seasonal water availability, with the majority of rainfall confined to one season. Savannas are associated with several types of biomes. Savannas are frequently in a transitional zone between forest and desert or prairie. Savanna covers approximately 20 per cent of the Earth's land area. The largest area of savanna is in Africa.

Although the term *savanna* is believed to have originally come from an Arawak word describing "land which is without trees but with much grass either tall or short" (Oviedo y Valdes, 1535), by the late 1800s it was used to mean "land with both grass and trees". It now refers to land with grass and either scattered trees or an open canopy of trees.

Spanish explorers familiar with the term 'sabana' called the grasslands they found around the Orinoco River 'llanos', as well as calling Venezuelan and Colombian grasslands by that specific term. 'Cerrado' was used on the higher savannas of the Brazilian Central Plateau.

Many grassy landscapes and mixed communities of trees, shrubs, and grasses were described as savanna before the middle of the 19th century, when the concept of a tropical savanna climate became established. The Köppen climate classification system was strongly influenced by effects of temperature and precipitation upon tree growth, and his over-simplified assumptions resulted in a tropical savanna classification concept which resulted in it being considered as a 'climatic climax' formation. The common usage meaning to describe vegetation now conflicts with a simplified yet widespread climatic concept meaning. The divergence has sometimes caused areas such as extensive savannas north and south of the Congo and Amazon Rivers to be excluded from mapped savanna categories.

'Barrens' has been used almost interchangeably with savanna in different parts of North America. Sometimes midwestern savanna were described as 'grassland with trees'. Different authors have defined the lower limits of savanna tree coverage as 5-10 per cent and upper limits range from 25-80 per cent of an area.

Two factors common to all savanna environments are rainfall variations from year to year, and dry season wildfires. Savannas around the world are also dominated by tropical grasses which use the C4 type of photosynthesis. In the Americas, *e.g.* in Belize, Central America, savanna vegetation is similar from Mexico to South America and to the Caribbean. In North America nearby trees are of subtropical types, ranging from southwestern Pinyon pine to southeastern Longleaf Pine and northern chestnut oak.

Savannas are subject to regular wildfires and the ecosystem appears to be the result of human use of fire. For example, Native Americans created the Pre-Columbian savannas of North America by periodically burning where fire-resistant plants were the dominant species. Pine barrens in scattered locations from New Jersey to coastal New England are remnants of these savannas. Aboriginal burning appears to have been responsible for the widespread occurrence of savanna in tropical Australia and New Guinea, and savannas in India are a result of human fire use. The maquis shrub savannas of the Mediterranean region were likewise created and maintained by anthropogenic fire.

These fires are usually confined to the herbaceous layer and do little long term damage to mature trees. However, these fires either kill or suppress tree seedlings, thus preventing the establishment of a continuous tree canopy which would prevent further grass growth. Prior to European settlement aboriginal land use practices, including fire, influenced vegetation and may have maintained and modified savanna flora. It has been suggested by many authors that aboriginal burning created a structurally more open savanna landscape. Aboriginal burning certainly created a habitat mosaic that probably increased biodiversity and changed the structure of woodlands and geographic range of numerous woodland species. t has been suggested by many authors that with the removal or alteration of traditional burning regimes many savannas are being replaced by forest and shrub thickets with little herbaceous layer.

The consumption of herbage by introduced grazers in savanna woodlands has led to a reduction in the amount of fuel available for burning and resulted in fewer and cooler fires. The introduction of exotic pasture legumes has also led to a reduction in the need to burn to produce a flush of green growth because legumes retain high nutrient levels throughout the year, and because fires can have a negative impact on legume populations which causes a reluctance to burn.

Grazing and Browsing Animals

The closed forests types such as broadleaf forests and rainforests are usually not grazed owing to the closed structure precluding grass growth, and hence offering little opportunity for grazing. In contrast the open structure of savannas allows the growth of a herbaceous layer and are commonly used for grazing domestic livestock. As a result much of the world's savannas have undergone change as a result of grazing by sheep, goats and cattle, ranging from changes in pasture composition to woody weed encroachment.

The removal of grass by grazing affects the woody plant component of woodland systems in two major ways. Grasses compete with woody plants for water in the topsoil and removal by grazing reduces this competitive effect, potentially boosting tree growth. In addition to this effect the removal of fuel reduces both the intensity and the frequency of fires which may control woody plant species. Grazing animals can have a more direct effect on woody plants by the browsing of palatable woody species. There is evidence that unpalatable woody plants have increased under grazing in savannas. Grazing also promotes the spread of weeds in savannas by the removal or reduction of the plants which would normally compete with potential weeds and hinder establishment. In addition to this, cattle and horses are implicated in the spread of the seeds of weed species such as Prickly Acacia (*Acacia nilotica*) and Stylo (*Stylosanthes* spp.). Alterations in savanna species composition brought about by grazing can alter ecosystem function, and are exacerbated by overgrazing and poor land management practices.

Introduced grazing animals can also affect soil condition through physical compaction and break-up of the soil caused by the hooves of animals and through the erosion effects caused by the removal of protective plant cover. Such effects are most likely to occur on land subjected to repeated and heavy grazing. The effects of overstocking are often worst on soils of low fertility and in low rainfall areas below 500 mm, as most soil nutrients in these areas tend to be concentrated in the surface so any movement of soils can lead to severe degradation. Alteration in soil structure and nutrient levels affects the establishment, growth and survival of plant species and in turn can lead to a change in woodland structure and composition.

Tree Clearing

Large areas of savanna have been cleared of trees, and this clearing is continuing today. For example until recently 480,000 ha of savanna were cleared annually in Australia alone primarily to improve pasture production. Substantial savanna areas have been cleared of woody vegetation and much of the area that remains today is vegetation that has been disturbed by either clearing or thinning at some point in the past.

Clearing is carried out by the grazing industry in an attempt to increase the quality and quantity of feed available for stock and to improve the management of livestock. The removal of trees from savanna land removes the competition for water from the grasses present, and can lead to a two to fourfold increase in pasture production, as well as improving the quality of the feed available. Since stock carrying capacity is strongly correlated with herbage yield there can be major financial benefits from the removal of trees. The removal of trees also assists grazing management. For example in sheep grazing regions of dense tree and shrub cover harbours predators, leading to increased stock losses while woody plant cover hinders mustering in both sheep and cattle areas.

A number of techniques have been employed to clear or kill woody plants in savannas. Early pastoralists used felling and girdling, the removal of a ring of bark and sapwood, as a means of clearing land. In the 1950s arboricides suitable for stem injection were developed. War-surplus heavy machinery was made available, and these were used for either pushing timber, or for pulling using a chain and ball strung between two machines. These two new methods of timber control, along with the introduction and widespread adoption of several new pasture grasses and legumes promoted a resurgence in tree clearing. The 1980s also saw the release of soil-applied arboricides, notably tebuthiuron, that could be utilised without cutting and injecting each individual tree.

In many ways 'artificial' clearing, particularly pulling, mimics the effects of fire and, in savannas adapted to regeneration after fire as most Queensland savannas are, there is a similar response to that after fire. Tree clearing in many savanna communities, although causing a dramatic reduction in basal area and canopy cover, often leaves a high percentage of woody plants alive either as seedlings too small to be affected or as plants capable of re-sprouting from lignotubers and broken stumps. A population of woody plants equal to half or more of the original number often remains following pulling of eucalypt communities, even if all the trees over five metres are uprooted completely.

Exotic Plant Species

A number of exotic plants species have been introduced to the savannas around the world. Amongst the woody plant species are serious environmental weeds such as Prickly Acacia (*Acacia nilotica*), Rubbervine (*Cryptostegia grandiflora*), Mesquite (*Prosopis* spp.), Lantana (*Lantana camara* and *L. montevidensis*) and Prickly Pear (*Opuntia* spp.) A range of herbaceous species have also been introduced to these woodlands, either deliberately or accidentally including Rhodes grass and other *Chloris* species, Buffel grass (*Cenchrus ciliaris*), Giant rat's tail grass (*Sporobolus pyramidalis*) parthenium (*Parthenium hysteropherus*) and stylos (*Stylosanthes* spp.) and other legumes. These introductions have the potential to significantly alter the structure and composition of savannas worldwide, and have already done so in many areas through a number of processes including altering the fire regime, increasing grazing pressure, competing with native vegetation and occupying previously vacant ecological niches. Other plant species include: white sage, spotted cactus, cotton seed, rosemary.

Climate Change

There exists the possibility that human induced climate change in the form of the greenhouse effect may result in an alteration of the structure and function of savannas. Some authors have suggested that savannas and grasslands may become even more susceptible to woody plant encroachment as a result of greenhouse induced climate change. However, a recent case described a savanna increasing its range at the expense of forest in response to climate variation, and potential exists for similar rapid, dramatic shifts in vegetation distribution as a result of global climate change, particularly at ecotones such as savannas so often represent.

Savanna Ecoregions

Savanna ecoregions are of several different types:

- ***Tropical and subtropical savannas*** are classified with tropical and subtropical grasslands and shrublands as the tropical and subtropical grasslands, savannas, and shrublands biome. The savannas of Africa, including the Serengeti, famous for its wildlife, are typical of this type.
- ***Temperate savannas*** are mid-latitude savannas with wetter summers and drier winters. They are classified with temperate savannas and shrublands as the temperate grasslands, savannas, and shrublands biome, that for example cover much of the Great Plains of the United States.
- ***Mediterranean savannas*** are mid-latitude savannas in Mediterranean climate regions, with mild, rainy winters and hot, dry summers, part of the Mediterranean forests, woodlands, and scrub biome. The oak tree savannas of California, part of the California chaparral and woodlands ecoregion, fall into this category.
- ***Flooded savannas*** are savannas that are flooded seasonally or year-round. They are classified with flooded savannas as the flooded grasslands and savannas biome, which occurs mostly in the tropics and subtropics.
- ***Montane*** savannas are high-altitude savannas, located in a few spots around the world's high mountain regions, part of the montane grasslands and shrublands biome.

The highland savannas of the Angolan Scarp savanna and woodlands ecoregion are an example.

Steppe

In physical geography, a steppe is an ecoregion, in the montane grasslands and shrublands and temperate grasslands, savannas, and shrublands biomes, characterized by grassland plains without trees apart from those near rivers and lakes. The prairie (especially the shortgrass and mixed prairie) is an example of a steppe, though it is not usually called such. It may be semi-desert, or covered with grass or shrubs or both, depending on the season and latitude. The term is also used to denote the climate encountered in regions too dry to support a forest, but not dry enough to be a desert. Soil type is typically chernozem.

Steppes are usually characterized by a semi-arid and continental climate. Extremes can be recorded in the summer of up to 40°C (104°F) and in winter, –40°C (–40°F). Besides this huge difference between summer and winter, the differences between day and night are also very great. In the highlands of Mongolia, 30°C (86°F) can be reached during the day with sub-zero°C (sub 32°F) readings at night.

The mid-latitude steppes can be summarised by hot summers and cold winters, averaging 250-500 mm (10-20 inches) of precipitation per year. Precipitation level alone is not what defines a steppe climate, potential evapotranspiration must also be taken into account.

Two types of steppe can be recorded:

1. *Temperate steppe:* the 'true' steppe, found in continental areas of the world; it can be further subdivided as seen here.
2. *Subtropical steppe:* a similar association of plants that can be found in the driest areas with a Mediterranean-like climate; it has usually a short wet period.

Peculiar types of steppe include shrub-steppe and alpine-steppe.

The world's largest steppe region, often referred to as 'the Great Steppe', is found in southwestern Russia and neighbouring countries in Central Asia, stretching from Ukraine in the west through Turkmenistan, Uzbekistan and Kazakhstan to the Altai, Koppet Dag and Tian Shan ranges.

The inner parts of Anatolia in Turkey, Central Anatolia and East Anatolia in particular and also some parts of Southeast Anatolia, as well as much of Armenia and Iran are largely dominated by cold steppe.

The Pannonian Plain is another steppe region in southeastern Europe, primarily Hungary.

Another large steppe area (prairie) is located in the central United States and western Canada. The shortgrass prairie steppe is the westernmost part of the Great Plains region. The Channeled Scablands in Southern British Columbia and Washington State are an example of a steppe region in North America outside of the Great Plains.

In South America, cold steppe can be found in Patagonia and much of the high elevation regions east of the southern Andes.

Relatively small steppe areas can be found in the interior of the South Island of New Zealand.

Subtropical Steppe

In Europe, some Mediterranean areas have a steppe-like vegetation, such as central Sicily, parts of Greece in the southern Athens area, and central-eastern Spain, especially the southeastern coast (around Murcia), and places cut off from adequate moisture due to rain shadow effects such as Zaragoza.

In Asia, a subtropical steppe can be found in semi-arid lands that fringe the Thar Desert of the Indian subcontinent.

In Australia, 'subtropical steppe' can found in a belt surrounding the most severe deserts of the continent and around the Musgrave Ranges. In North America this environment is typical of transition areas between zones with a Mediterranean climate and true deserts, such as Reno, Nevada, the inner part of California, and much of West Texas and adjacent areas in Mexico.

In South America the most important zone with a warm steppe is the Pampa.

Tropical Grasslands and Shrublands Similar to Steppe

Other zones dominated by grasslands and shrublands similar to steppe can be found in tropical areas of the world. In these locations, necessary rainfall to separate steppes from true deserts may be half as much again due to greater evapotranspiration. These include transition zones between savanna and severe desert such as the Sahel that fringes the true Sahara.

Another significant 'tropical steppe', noteworthy for not grading into desert, is the Sertão of northeastern Brazil.

CHAPTER – 3

Taiga and Tundra

Taiga, also known as the boreal forest, is a biome characterized by coniferous forests.

Taiga is the world's largest terrestrial biome and covers: in North America most of inland Canada and Alaska as well as parts of the extreme northern continental United States (especially northern Minnesota, Michigan's Upper Peninsula, northern Wisconsin, Upstate New York, Vermont, New Hampshire, and Maine); and in Eurasia most of Sweden, Finland, inland and northern Norway, much of Russia (especially Siberia), northern Kazakhstan, northern Mongolia, and northern Japan (on the island of Hokkaido).

The term *boreal forest* is sometimes, particularly in Canada, used to refer to the more southerly part of the biome, while the term taiga is often used to describe the more barren areas of the northernmost part of the taiga approaching the tree line.

Taiga is the world's largest land biome, and makes up 27 per cent of the world's forest cover; the largest areas are located in Russia and Canada. The taiga is the terrestrial biome with the lowest annual average temperatures after the tundra and permanent ice caps. However, extreme minimums in the taiga are typically lower than those of the tundra. The lowest reliably recorded temperatures in the Northern Hemisphere were recorded in the taiga of northeastern Russia. The taiga or boreal forest has a subarctic climate with very large temperature range between seasons, but the long and cold winter is the dominant feature. This climate is classified as *Dfc*, *Dwc*, *Dsc*, *Dfd*, *Dwd* and *Dsd* in the Köppen climate classification scheme, meaning that the short summer (24-hr average 10°C or more) lasts 1-3 months and always less than 4 months. There are also some much smaller areas grading towards the oceanic *Cfc* climate with milder winters. The mean annual temperature generally varies from -5°C to 5°C, but there are taiga areas in both eastern Siberia and interior Alaska-Yukon where the mean annual reaches down to -10°C. According to some sources, the boreal forest grades into a temperate mixed forest when mean annual temperature reaches about 3°C. Permafrost is common in areas with mean annual temperature below 0°C. The winters last 5-7 months, with average temperatures below freezing. Temperatures vary from -54°C to 30°C (-65°F to 86°F) throughout the whole year.The summers, while short, are generally warm and humid. In much of the taiga, -20°C would be a typical winter day temperature and 18°C an average summer day.

The growing season, when the vegetation in the taiga comes alive, is usually slightly longer than the climatic definition of summer as the plants of the boreal biome have a lower threshold to trigger growth. In Canada, Scandinavia and Finland, the growing season is often estimated by using the period of the year when the 24-hr average temperature is 5°C or more. For the Taiga Plains in Canada, growing season varies from 80 to 150 days, and in the Taiga Shield from 100 to 140 days. Some sources claim 130 days growing season as typical for the taiga. Other sources mention that 50-100 frost-free days are characteristic. Data for locations in southwest Yukon gives 80-120 frost-free days. The closed canopy boreal forest in Kenozersky near Plesetsk, Arkhangelsk Province, Russia, on average has 108 frost-free days. The longest growing season is found in the smaller areas with oceanic influences; in coastal areas of Scandinavia and Finland, the growing season of the closed boreal forest can be 145-180 days. The shortest growing season is found at the northern taiga-tundra ecotone, where the northern taiga forest no longer can grow and the tundra dominates the landscape when the growing season is down to 50-70 days, and the 24-hr average of the warmest month of the year usually is 10°C or less. High latitudes mean that the sun does not rise far above the horizon, and less solar energy is received than further south. But the high latitude also ensures very long summer days, as the sun stays above the horizon nearly 20 hours each day, with only around 6 hours of daylight occurring in the dark winters, depending on latitude. The areas of the taiga inside the Arctic circle have midnight sun in mid-summer and polar night in mid-winter.

The taiga experiences relatively low precipitation throughout the year (generally 200-750 mm annually, 1,000 mm in some areas), primarily as rain during the summer months, but also as fog and snow. As evaporation is also low for most of the year, precipitation exceeds evaporation, and is sufficient to sustain the dense vegetation growth. Snow may remain on the ground for as long as nine months in the northernmost extensions of the taiga ecozone.

In general, taiga grows to the south of the 10°C July isotherm, but occasionally as far north as the 9°C July isotherm. The southern limit is more variable, depending on rainfall; taiga may be replaced by forest steppe south of the 15°C July isotherm where rainfall is very low, but more typically extends south to the 18°C July isotherm, and locally where rainfall is higher (notably in eastern Siberia and adjacent northern Manchuria) south to the 20°C July isotherm. In these warmer areas the taiga has higher species diversity, with more warmth-loving species such as Korean Pine, Jezo Spruce, and Manchurian Fir, and merges gradually into mixed temperate forest or, more locally (on the Pacific Ocean coasts of North America and Asia), into coniferous temperate rainforests.

Much of the area currently classified as taiga was recently glaciated. As the glaciers receded they left depressions in the topography that have since filled with water, creating lakes and bogs (especially muskeg soil) found throughout the taiga.

Taiga soil tends to be young and poor in nutrients. It lacks the deep, organically-enriched profile present in temperate deciduous forests. The thinness of the soil is due largely to the cold, which hinders the development of soil and the ease with which plants can use its nutrients. Fallen leaves and moss can remain on the forest floor for a long time in the cool, moist climate, which limits their organic contribution to the soil; acids from evergreen needles further leach the soil, creating spodosol. Since the soil is acidic due to the falling pine needles, the forest floor has only lichens and some mosses growing on it.

Since North America and Asia used to be connected by the Bering land bridge, a number of animal and plant species (more animals than plants) were able to colonize both continents and are distributed throughout the taiga biome. Others differ regionally, typically with each genus having several distinct species, each occupying different regions of the taiga. Taigas also have some small-leaved deciduous trees like birch, alder, willow, and poplar; mostly in areas escaping the most extreme winter cold. However, the Dahurian Larch tolerates the coldest winters in the northern hemisphere in eastern Siberia. The very southernmost parts of the taiga may have trees such as oak, maple, elm, and tilia scattered among the conifers, and there is usually a gradual transition into a temperate mixed forest, such as the Eastern forest-boreal transition of eastern Canada. In the interior of the continents with the driest climate, the boreal forests might grade into temperate grassland.

There are two major types of taiga. The southern part is the closed canopy forest, consisting of many closely-spaced trees with mossy ground cover. In clearings in the forest, shrubs and wildflowers are common, such as the fireweed. The other type is the lichen woodland or sparse taiga, with trees that are farther-spaced and lichen ground cover; the latter is common in the northernmost taiga. In the northernmost taiga the forest cover is not only more sparse, but often stunted in growth form; moreover, ice pruned asymmetric Black Spruce (in North America) are often seen, with diminished foliage on the windward side. In Canada, Scandinavia and Finland, the boreal forest is usually divided into three subzones: The high boreal (north boreal) or taiga zone; the middle boreal (closed forest); and the southern boreal, a closed canopy boreal forest with some scattered temperate deciduous trees among the conifers, such as maple, elm and oak. This southern boreal forest has the longest and warmest growing season of the biome, and in some regions (including Scandinavia, Finland and western Russia) this subzone is commonly used for agricultural purposes. The boreal forest is home to many types of berries; some are confined to the southern and middle closed boreal forest (such as raspberry), others grow in most areas of the taiga (such as cranberry and cloudberry), and some can grow in both the taiga and the low arctic (southern part of) tundra (such as bilberry and lingonberry). The forests of the taiga are largely coniferous, dominated by larch, spruce, fir, and pine. The woodland mix varies according to geography and climate so for example the Eastern Canadian forests ecoregion of the higher elevations of the Laurentian Mountains and the northern Appalachian Mountains in Canada is dominated by balsam fir *Abies balsamea*, while further north the Eastern Canadian Shield taiga of northern Quebec and Labrador is notably black spruce *Picea mariana* and tamarack larch *Larix laricina*.

Evergreen species in the taiga (spruce, fir, and pine) have a number of adaptations specifically for survival in harsh taiga winters, although larch, the most cold-tolerant of all trees, is deciduous. Taiga trees tend to have shallow roots to take advantage of the thin soils, while many of them seasonally alter their biochemistry to make them more resistant to freezing, called 'hardening'. The narrow conical shape of northern conifers, and their downward-drooping limbs, also help them shed snow.

Because the sun is low in the horizon for most of the year, it is difficult for plants to generate energy from photosynthesis. Pine, spruce and fir do not lose their leaves seasonally and are able to photosynthesize with their older leaves in late winter and spring when light is good but temperatures are still too low for new growth to commence. The adaptation of evergreen needles limits the water lost due to transpiration and their dark green colour increases their absorption of sunlight. Although precipitation is not a limiting factor, the ground freezes during the winter months and plant roots are unable to absorb water, so desiccation can be a severe problem in late winter for evergreens.

Although the taiga is dominated by coniferous forests, some broadleaf trees also occur, notably birch, aspen, willow, and rowan. Many smaller herbaceous plants grow closer to the ground. Periodic stand-replacing wildfires (with return times of between 20-200 years) clear out the tree canopies, allowing sunlight to invigorate new growth on the forest floor. For some species, wildfires are a necessary part of the life cycle in the taiga; some, *e.g.* Jack Pine have cones which only open to release their seed after a fire, dispersing their seeds onto the newly cleared ground. Grasses grow wherever they can find a patch of sun, and mosses and lichens thrive on the damp ground and on the sides of tree trunks. In comparison with other biomes, however, the taiga has low biological diversity.

Coniferous trees are the dominant plants of the taiga biome. A very few species in four main genera are found: the evergreen spruce, fir, and pine, and the deciduous larch. In North America, one or two species of fir and one or two species of spruce are dominant. Across Scandinavia and western

Russia, the Scots pine is a common component of the taiga, while taiga of the Russian Far East and Mongolia is dominated by larch.

Fauna

The boreal forest, or taiga, supports a large range of animals. Canada's boreal forest includes 85 species of mammals, 130 species of fish, and an estimated 32,000 species of insects. Insects play a critical role as pollinators, decomposers, and as a part of the food chain. Many nesting birds rely on them for food. The cold winters and short summers make the taiga a challenging biome for reptiles and amphibians, which depend on environmental conditions to regulate their body temperatures, and there are only a few species in the boreal forest. Some hibernate underground in winter.

The taiga is home to a number of large herbivorous mammals, such as moose and reindeer/caribou. Some areas of the more southern closed boreal forest also have populations of other deer species such as the elk (wapiti) and roe deer. There is also a range of rodent species including beaver, squirrel, mountain hare, snowshoe hare, and vole. These species have evolved to survive the harsh winters in their native ranges. Some larger mammals, such as bears, eat heartily during the summer in order to gain weight, and then go into hibernation during the winter. Other animals have adapted layers of fur or feathers to insulate them from the cold.

A number of wildlife species threatened or endangered with extinction can be found in the Canadian boreal forest, including woodland caribou, American black bear, grizzly bear, and wolverine. Habitat loss, mainly due to logging, is the primary cause of decline for these species.

Due to the climate, carnivorous diets are an inefficient means of obtaining energy; energy is limited, and most energy is lost between trophic levels. Predatory birds (owls and eagles) and other smaller carnivores, including foxes and weasels, feed on the rodents. Larger carnivores, such as lynx and wolves, prey on the larger animals. Omnivores, such as bears and raccoons are fairly common, sometimes picking through human garbage.

More than 300 species of birds have their nesting grounds in the taiga. Siberian Thrush, White-throated Sparrow, and Black-throated Green Warbler migrate to this habitat to take advantage of the long summer days and abundance of insects found around the numerous bogs and lakes. Of the 300 species of birds that summer in the taiga only 30 stay for the winter. These are either carrion-feeding or large raptors that can take live mammal prey, including Golden Eagle, Rough-legged Buzzard (also known as the Rough-legged Hawk), and Raven, or else seed-eating birds, including several species of grouse and crossbills.

Large areas of Siberia's taiga have been harvested for lumber since the collapse of the Soviet Union. In Canada, eight per cent of the boreal forest is protected from development, the provincial government allows forest management to occur on Crown land under rigorous constraints. The main forestry practice in the boreal forest of Canada is clearcutting, which involves cutting down most of the trees in a given area, then replanting the forest as a monocrop (one species of tree) the following season. Industry officials claim that this process emulates the natural effects of a forest fire, which they claim clearcutting suppresses, protecting infrastructure, communities and roads. However, from an ecological perspective, this is a falsehood, for several reasons, including:

(a) Removing most of the trees in a given area is usually done using large machines which disrupt the soil greatly, and the dramatic diminution of ground cover permits large-scale erosion and avalanches, which further damage the habitat and sometimes engangers infra-structure, roads and communities;

(b) Clearcutting removes most of the biomass from an area, and the various macro and micro-nutrients it contains. This sudden decrease in nutrients in an area, contrasts with a forest fire, which returns most of the nutrients to the soil;

(c) Forest fires leave standing snags, and leave patches of unburned trees.

This helps preserve structure and micro-habitats within the area, whereas clearcutting destroys most of these habitats. In the past, clearcuts upwards of 110 km^2 have been recorded in the Canadian boreal forest. However, today 80 per cent of clearcuts are less than 260 hectares (2.6 square km). Some of the products from logged boreal forests include toilet paper, copy paper, newsprint, and lumber. More than 90 per cent of boreal forest products from Canada are exported for consumption and processing in the United States, however with the recession and fewer US homes being built that has changed. Some of the larger cities situated in this biome are Murmansk, Arkhangelsk, Yakutsk, Anchorage, Yellowknife, Tromsø, Luleå, and Oulu.

Most companies that harvest in Canadian forests are certified by an independent third party agency such as the Forest Stewardship Council (FSC), Sustainable Forests Initiative (SFI), or the Canadian Standards Association (CSA). While the certification process differs between these groups, all of them include forest stewardship, respect for aboriginal peoples, compliance with local, provincial or national environmental laws, forest worker safety, education and training, and other environmental, business, and social requirements. The prompt renewal of all harvest sites by planting or natural renewal is also required.

Climate Change

The zone of latitude occupied by the boreal forest has experienced some of the greatest temperature increases on Earth, especially during the last quarter of the twentieth century. Winter temperatures have increased more than summer temperatures. The number of days with extremely cold temperatures (*e.g.*, -20 to -40°C) has decreased irregularly but systematically in nearly all the boreal region, allowing better survival for tree-damaging insects. In summer, the daily low temperature has increased more than the daily high temperature. In Fairbanks, Alaska, the length of the frost-free season has increased from 60-90 days in the early twentieth century to about 120 days a century later. Summer warming has been shown to increased water stress and reduce tree growth in dry areas of the southern boreal forest in central Alaska, western Canada and portions of far eastern Russia. Precipitation is relatively abundant in Scandinavia, Finland, northwest Russia and eastern Canada, where warmer summers accelerate tree growth. As a consequence of this warming trend, the warmer parts of the boreal forests are susceptible to replacement by grassland, parkland or temperate forest. In Siberia, the taiga is converting from predominantly needle-shedding larch trees to evergreen conifers in response to a warming climate. This is likely to further accelerate warming, as the evergreen trees will absorb more of the sun's rays. Given the vast size of the area, such a change has the potential to affect areas well outside of the region. In much of the boreal forest in Alaska, the growth of white spruce trees are stunted by unusually warm summers, while trees on some of the coldest fringes of the forest are experiencing faster growth than previously. Lack of moisture in the warmer summers are also stressing the birch trees of central Alaska. Many nations are taking direct steps to protect the ecology of the taiga by prohibiting logging, mining, oil and gas production, and other forms of development. In February 2010 the Canadian government established protection for 13,000 square kilometres of boreal forest by creating a new 10,700 square kilometre park reserve in the Mealy Mountains area of eastern Canada and a 3,000 square kilometre waterway provincial park that follows alongside the Eagle River from headwaters to sea. The taiga stores enormous quantities of carbon, possibly more than the temperate and tropical forests combined, much of it in peatland.

One of the biggest areas of research and a topic still full of unsolved questions is the recurring disturbance of fire and the role it plays in propagating the lichen woodland. The phenomenon of wildfire by lightning strike is the primary determinant of understory vegetation and because of this, it is considered to be predominate driving force behind community and ecosystem properties in the lichen woodland. The significance of fire is clearly evident when one considers that understory vegetation influences tree seedling germination in the short term and decomposition of biomass and nutrient availability in the long term. The recurrent cycle of large, damaging fire occurs approximately every 70 to 100 years. Understanding the dynamics of this ecosystem is entangled with discovering the successional paths that the vegetation exhibits after a fire. Trees, shrubs and lichens all recover from fire induced damage through vegetative reproduction as well as invasion by propagules. Seeds that have fallen and become buried provide little help in re-establishment of a species. The reappearance of lichens is reasoned to occur because of varying conditions and light/ nutrient availability in each different microstate. Several different studies have been done that have led to the formation of the theory that post-fire development can be propagated by any of four pathways: self replacement, species-dominance relay, species replacement, or gap-phase self replacement. Self replacement is simply the re-establishment of the pre-fire dominant species. Species-dominance relay is a sequential attempt of tree species to establish dominance in the canopy. Species replacement is when fires occur in sufficient frequency to interrupt species dominance relay. Gap-Phase Self-Replacement is the least common and so far has only been documented in Western Canada. It is a self replacement of the surviving species into the canopy gaps after a fire kills another species. The particular pathway taken after a fire disturbance depends on how the landscape is able to support trees as well as fire frequency. Fire frequency has a large role in shaping the original inception of the lower forest line of the lichen woodland taiga.

Centuries ago, the southern limits of lichen woodland taiga were only being formed It has been hypothesized and subsequently proved by Serge Payette that the Spruce-Moss forest ecosystem was changed into the lichen woodland biome due to the initiation of two compounded strong disturbances. The two disturbances were large fire and the appearance and attack of the spruce budworm. The spruce budworm is a deadly insect to the spruce populations in the southern regions of the taiga. J.P. Jasinski confirmed this theory five years later stating "Their [lichen woodlands] persistence , along with their previous moss forest histories and current occurrence adjacent to closed moss forests, indicate that they are an alternative stable state to the spruce–moss forests".

Tundra

In physical geography, tundra is a biome where the tree growth is hindered by low temperatures and short growing seasons. The term *tundra* comes through Russian from the Kildin Sami word *tundâr* 'uplands', 'treeless mountain tract'. There are three types of tundra:

1. Arctic tundra;
2. Alpine tundra; and
3. Antarctic tundra.

In tundra, the vegetation is composed of dwarf shrubs, sedges and grasses, mosses, and lichens. Scattered trees grow in some tundra. The ecotone (or ecological boundary region) between the tundra and the forest is known as the tree line or timberline.

Arctic tundra occurs in the far Northern Hemisphere, north of the taiga belt. The word 'tundra' usually refers only to the areas where the subsoil is permafrost, or permanently frozen soil. (It may also refer to the treeless plain in general, so that northern Sápmi would be included.) Permafrost tundra includes vast areas of northern Russia and Canada. The polar tundra is home to several peoples who are mostly nomadic reindeer herders, such as the Nganasan and Nenets in the permafrost area (and the Sami in Sápmi).

Arctic tundra contains areas of stark landscape and is frozen for much of the year. The soil there is frozen from 25-90 cm (9.8-35.4 inches) down, and it is impossible for trees to grow. Instead, bare and sometimes rocky land can only support low growing plants such as moss, heath (Ericaceae varieties such as crowberry and black bearberry), and lichen. There are two main seasons, winter and summer, in the polar tundra areas. During the winter it is very cold and dark, with the average temperature around -28°C (-18°F), sometimes dipping as low as -50°C (-58°F). However, extreme cold temperatures on the tundra do not drop as low as those experienced in taiga areas further south (for example, Russia's and Canada's lowest temperatures were recorded in locations south of the tree line). During the summer, temperatures rise somewhat, and the top layer of the permafrost melts, leaving the ground very soggy. The tundra is covered in marshes, lakes, bogs and streams during the warm months. Generally daytime temperatures during the summer rise to about 12°C (54°F) but can often drop to 3°C (37°F) or even below freezing. Arctic tundras are sometimes the subject of habitat conservation programmes. In Canada and Russia, many of these areas are protected through a national Biodiversity Action Plan.

The tundra is a very windy area, with winds often blowing upwards of 48-97 km/h (30-60 miles an hour). However, in terms of precipitation, it is desert-like, with only about 15-25 cm (6-10 inches) falling per year (the summer is typically the season of maximum precipitation). During the summer, the permafrost thaws just enough to let plants grow and reproduce, but because the ground below this is frozen, the water cannot sink any lower, and so the water forms the lakes and marshes found during the summer months. Although precipitation is light, evaporation is also relatively minimal.

The biodiversity of the tundras is low: 1,700 species of vascular plants and only 48 land mammals can be found, although millions of birds migrate there each year for the marshes. There are also a few fish species such as the flatfish. There are few species with large populations. Notable animals in the Arctic tundra include caribou (reindeer), musk ox, arctic hare, arctic fox, snowy owl, lemmings, and polar bears (only the extreme north).

Due to the harsh climate of the Arctic tundra, regions of this kind have seen little human activity, even though they are sometimes rich in natural resources such as oil and uranium. In recent times this has begun to change in Alaska, Russia, and some other parts of the world.

A severe threat to the tundras, specifically to the permafrost, is global warming. The melting of the permafrost in a given area on human time scales (decades or centuries) could radically change which species can survive there.

Another concern is that about one third of the world's soil-bound carbon is in taiga and tundra areas. When the permafrost melts, it releases carbon in the form of carbon dioxide and methane, both of which are greenhouse gases. The effect has been observed in Alaska. In the 1970s the tundra was a carbon sink, but today, it is a carbon source.

Antarctic tundra occurs on Antarctica and on several Antarctic and subantarctic islands, including South Georgia and the South Sandwich Islands and the Kerguelen Islands. Most of Antarctica is too cold and dry to support vegetation, and most of the continent is covered by ice fields. However, some portions of the continent, particularly the Antarctic Peninsula, have areas of rocky soil that support plant life. The flora presently consists of around 300-400 lichens, 100 mosses, 25 liverworts, and around 700 terrestrial and aquatic algae species, which live on the areas of exposed rock and soil around the shore of the continent. Antarctica's two flowering plant species, the Antarctic hair grass (*Deschampsia antarctica*) and Antarctic pearlwort (*Colobanthus quitensis*), are found on the northern and western parts of the Antarctic Peninsula.

In contrast with the Arctic tundra, the Antarctic tundra lacks a large mammal fauna, mostly due to its physical isolation from the other continents. Sea mammals and sea birds, including seals and penguins, inhabit areas near the shore, and some small mammals, like rabbits and cats, have been introduced by humans to some of the subantarctic islands. The Antipodes Subantarctic Islands tundra ecoregion includes the Bounty Islands, Auckland Islands, Antipodes Islands, the Campbell Island group, and Macquarie Island. Species endemic to this ecoregion include *Nematoceras dienemum* and *Nematoceras sulcatum*, the only Subantarctic orchids; the royal penguin; and the Antipodean albatross.

The flora and fauna of Antarctica and the Antarctic Islands (south of 60° south latitude) are protected by the Antarctic Treaty.

Alpine tundra does not contain trees because it has high altitude. Alpine tundra is distinguished from arctic tundra, because alpine tundra typically does not have permafrost, and alpine soils are generally better drained than arctic soils. Alpine tundra transitions to subalpine forests below the tree line; stunted forests occurring at the forest-tundra ecotone are known as *Krummholz.*

Alpine tundra occurs in mountains worldwide. The flora of the alpine tundra is characterized by dwarf shrubs close to the ground. The cold climate of the alpine tundra is caused by the low air pressure, and is similar to polar climate.

Tundra climates ordinarily fit the Köppen climate classification ET, signifying a local climate in which at least one month has an average temperature high enough to melt snow (0°C or 32°F), but no month with an average temperature in excess of (10°C/50°F). The cold limit generally meets the EF climates of permanent ice and snows; the warm-summer limit generally corresponds with the poleward or altitudinal limit of trees, where they grade into the subarctic climates designated Dfd and Dwd (extreme winters as in parts of Siberia), Dfc typical in Alaska, Canada, European Russia, and Western Siberia (cold winters with months of freezing), or even Cfc (no month colder than -3°C as in parts of Iceland and southernmost South America). Tundra climates as a rule are hostile to woody vegetation even where the winters are comparatively mild by polar standards, as in Iceland.

Despite the potential diversity of climates in the ET category involving precipitation, extreme temperatures, and relative wet and dry seasons, this category is rarely subdivided. Rainfall and snowfall are generally slight due to the low vapor pressure of water in the chilly atmosphere, but as a rule potential evapotranspiration is extremely low, allowing soggy terrain of swamps and bogs even in places that get precipitation typical of deserts of lower and middle latitudes. The amount of native tundra biomass depends more on the local temperature than the amount of precipitation.

Veld

The term Veld (often spelled Veldt) refers primarily (but not exclusively) to the wide open rural spaces of South Africa or southern Africa and in particular to certain flatter areas or districts covered in grass or low scrub. The word *veld* comes from the Afrikaans (ultimately from Dutch), literally meaning 'field'.

However, this simple translation does not convey the subtleties of the many idiomatic nuances and technical applications of the term. A typical authoritative dictionary will devote columns, or even pages to the subject . Veld can be compared to the Australian terms 'outback' or 'bush', to 'the prairie' of North America, or to the 'pampas' of South

America but the comparisons are not exact. A Yorkshireman might equate 'wandering across the moors' to 'walking through the veld'.

By extension, the veld can be compared to 'the boondocks' or those places 'beyond the black stump' in Australia. There is a sense in which it refers in essence to unimproved land (and is therefore not the equivalent of the English 'paddock') and does not include areas used both for pastoral activities and the planting of crops. These areas are referred to as fields. The word is less appropriate for land that is heavily forested, mountainous, or urban. The simplest explanation will be to say the word 'veld' means 'natural vegetation'; excluding vegetation like swamps and forests. It does include mountains with vegetation but not deserts or mountains without natural vegetation. (On the other hand, a carefully husbanded sports field on which the game of Rugby is played in the middle of cities such as Cape Town or Johannesburg is referred to as a 'rugbyveld' in the Afrikaans language). Whereas mountainous peaks and forests are not really welcomed on the veld, bushes are acceptable. The area then becomes 'bosveld'. There are minor examples of bosveld here and there but the term is used mainly to describe Die Bosveld ('The Bushveld'), which is both a loose botanical classification and a specific geographical part of what used to be known as the Transvaal.

The word 'veld' also carries military connotations. The word 'field' in English has a strong association with 'war', as evidenced by the expression 'the first foe in the field' and the lines of the ballad 'Lord Marlborough' "You generals all and champions bold, that takes delight in field, that knocks down churches and castle walls but now to death must yield". The same relationship is paralleled in Afrikaans. Just as the English Army has its Field Marshals, the Boer armies had their Veldkornets and Veldkommandos.

Much of the interior of southern Africa consists of a high plateau known as the Highveld, starting east of the

Johannesburg centre. These higher, cooler areas (generally more than 5000 ft [1524m] above sea level) are characterised by flat or gently undulating terrain, grasslands and a modified tropical or subtropical climate. In some areas there is a distinct escarpment bordering the plateau, while in others the boundary is not obvious.

Some surrounding, lower areas are known as Lowveld and are generally hotter and less intensely cultivated. Before the middle of the 20th century, much of the Lowveld was home to the tsetse fly, which transmits sleeping sickness. These areas used to be known as 'fever country' and were avoided by mounted travellers, owing to the susceptibility of horses to a form of the disease. Malaria was in the past also a major problem in the hotter parts of the Lowveld.This disease is caused by mosqitoes.

Quote

"How well I remember the years I spent tending the cattle on the large farm, roaming over all its far expanse of veld, in which every kloof, every valley, every koppie was endeared to me by the most familiar associations. Month after month I had spent there in lonely occupation—alone with the cattle, myself and God. The veld had grown part of me, not only in the sense that my bones were a part of it, but in that more vital sense which identifies nature with man ... Having no human companion, I felt a spirit of comradeship for the objects around me. In my childish way I communed with these as with my own soul; they became the sharers of my confidence.

CHAPTER – 4

Poaceae

Poaceae (formerly known as Gramineae) is a family in the Class Liliopsida (the monocots) of the flowering plants. Plants of this family are usually called grasses, or, to distinguish them from other graminoids, true grasses; the shrub- or tree-like plants in this family are called bamboo (there are also herbaceous, non-woody bamboos). There are about 600 genera and some 9,000-10,000 or more species of grasses (Kew Index of World Grass Species).

Plant communities dominated by Poaceae are called grasslands; it is estimated that grasslands comprise 20 per cent of the vegetation cover of the Earth. Grass species also occur in many other habitats that are not formally considered to be grasslands, including different types of wetlands (*e.g.*, fens, marshes), forests and tundra.

Poaceae is often considered to be the most important of all plant families to human economies: it includes the staple food grains and cereal crops grown around the world, lawn and forage grasses, and bamboo, which is widely used for construction throughout east Asia and sub-Saharan Africa. Civilization was founded largely on the ability to domesticate cereal grass crops around the world.

The term 'grass' is also applied to plants that are not members of the Poaceae lineage, including the rushes (Juncaceae) and sedges (Cyperaceae). This broad and general use of the word 'grass' has led to plants of the Poaceae often being called 'true grasses'.

Poaceae have hollow stems called *culms*, which are plugged (solid) at intervals called *nodes*, the points along the culm at which leaves arise. Grass leaves are alternate, *distichous* (in one plane) or rarely spiral, and parallel-veined. Each leaf is differentiated into a lower *sheath* which hugs the stem for a distance and a *blade* with margins usually entire. The leaf blades of many grasses are hardened with silica phytoliths, which helps discourage grazing animals. In some grasses (such as sword grass) this makes the edges of the grass blades sharp enough to cut human skin. A membranous appendage or fringe of hairs, called the *ligule*, lies at the junction between sheath and blade, preventing water or insects from penetrating into the sheath.

Grass blades grow at the base of the blade and not from elongated stem tips. This low growth point evolved in response to grazing animals and allows grasses to be grazed or mown regularly without severe damage to the plant.

Flowers of Poaceae are characteristically arranged in *spikelets*, each spikelet having one or more florets (the spikelets are further grouped into panicles or spikes). A spikelet consists of two (or sometimes fewer) bracts at the base, called *glumes*, followed by one or more florets. A floret consists of the flower surrounded by two bracts called the *lemma* (the external one) and the *palea* (the internal). The flowers are usually hermaphroditic (maize, monoecious, is an exception) and pollination is always anemophilous, that is, by wind. The perianth is reduced to two scales, called *lodicules*, that expand and contract to spread the lemma and palea; these are generally interpreted to be modified sepals. This complex structure can be seen in the image on the left, portraying a wheat (*Triticum aestivum*) spike.

The fruit of Poaceae is a *caryopsis*, in which the seed coat is fused to the fruit wall and thus, not separable from it (as in a maize kernel).

There are three general classifications of growth habit present in grasses; bunch-type (also called caespitose), stoloniferous, and rhizomatous.

The success of the grasses lies in part in their morphology and growth processes, and in part in their physiological diversity. Most of the grasses divide into two physiological groups, using the C3 and C4 photosynthetic pathways for carbon fixation. The C4 grasses have a photosynthetic pathway linked to specialized Kranz leaf anatomy that particularly adapts them to hot climates and an atmosphere low in carbon dioxide.

C3 grasses are referred to as 'cool season grasses' while C4 plants are considered 'warm season grasses'. Grasses may be either annual or perennial.

- *Annual Cool Season* — wheat, rye, Annual Bluegrass (annual meadowgrass, *Poa annua*), and oat
- *Perennial Cool Season* — orchardgrass (cocksfoot, *Dactylis glomerata*), fescue (*Festuca* spp), Kentucky Bluegrass and perennial ryegrass (*Lolium perenne*)
- *Annual Warm Season* — corn, sudangrass, and pearl millet
- *Perennial Warm Season* — big bluestem, indiangrass, bermudagrass and switchgrass.

Grass Evolution

Until recently grasses were thought to have evolved around 55 million years ago, based on fossil records. However, recent findings of 65-million-year-old phytoliths resembling grass phytoliths (including ancestors of rice and bamboo) in Cretaceous dinosaur coprolites, may place the diversification of grasses to an earlier date.

The most recent classification of the grass family recognizes twelve subfamilies:

- Anomochlooideae, a small lineage of broad-leaved grasses that includes two genera (*Anomochloa*, *Streptochaeta*)
- Pharoideae, a small lineage of grasses that includes three genera, including *Pharus* and *Leptaspis*
- Puelioideae, a small lineage that includes the African genus *Puelia.*
- Pooideae, including wheat, barley, oats, brome-grass (*Bromus*), reed-grasses (*Calamagrostis*) and many lawn and pasture grasses
- Bambusoideae, including bamboo
- Ehrhartoideae, including rice, wild rice
- Arundinoideae, including giant reed, common reed
- Centothecoideae, a small subfamily of 11 genera that is sometimes included in Panicoideae
- Chloridoideae, including the lovegrasses (*Eragrostis*, ca. 350 species, including teff), dropseeds (*Sporobolus*, some 160 species), inger millet (*Eleusine coracana* (L.) Gaertn.), and the muhly grasses (*Muhlenbergia*, ca. 175 species)
- Panicoideae, including panic grass, maize, sorghum, sugar cane, most millets, fonio, and bluestem grasses
- Micrairoideae
- Danthonioideae, including pampas grass

Poa is a Pooideae genus of about 500 species of grasses, native to the temperate regions of both hemispheres.

Grasses are, in human terms, perhaps the most economically important plant family. Grasses' economic importance stems from several areas, including food production, industry, and lawns.

Food Production

Agricultural grasses grown for their edible seeds are called *cereals.* Three cereals — rice, wheat, and maize (corn)

— provide more than half of all calories eaten by humans. Of all crops, 70 per cent are grasses. Cereals constitute the major source of carbohydrate for humans and perhaps the major source of protein, and include rice in southern and eastern Asia, maize in Central and South America, and wheat and barley in Europe, northern Asia and the Americas.

Sugarcane is the major source of sugar production. Many other grasses are grown for forage and fodder for animal food, particularly for sheep and cattle, thereby indirectly providing more human calories.

Industry

Grasses are used for construction. Scaffolding made from bamboo is able to withstand typhoon force winds that would break steel scaffolding. Larger bamboos and *Arundo donax* have stout culms that can be used in a manner similar to timber, and grass roots stabilize the sod of sod houses. *Arundo* is used to make reeds for woodwind instruments, and bamboo is used for innumerable implements.

Grass fibre can be used for making paper, and for biofuel production.

Phragmites australis (common reed) is important in water treatment, wetland habitat preservation and land reclamation in the Old World.

Lawn and Ornamental Grasses

Grasses are the primary plant used in lawns, which themselves derive from grazed grasslands in Europe. They are also provide an important means of erosion control (*e.g.*, along roadsides), especially on sloping land.

Although supplanted by artificial turf in some games, grasses are still an important covering of playing surfaces in many sports, including football, tennis, golf, cricket, and softball/baseball.

Ornamental grasses, such as perennial bunch grasses, are used in many styles of garden design for their foliage, inflorescences, seed heads, and slope stabilization. They are often used in natural landscaping, xeriscaping, contemporary or modern landscaping, wildlife gardening, and native plant gardening.

With 10,025 known species, the Poaceae is the fourth largest plant family. Only Orchidaceae, Asteraceae, and Fabaceae have more species, although with over 10,000 species the Rubiaceae is not far behind.

Biomes dominated by grasses are called grasslands. If only large contiguous chunks of grasslands are counted, these biomes cover 31 per cent of the planet's land. Grasslands go by various names depending on location, including pampas, plains, steppes, or prairie.

In addition to their use as forage worldwide by many grazing mammals such as cattle and other livestock, deer, and elephants, grasses are used as food plants by many species of butterflies and moths; see List of Lepidoptera that feed on grasses.

The evolution of large grazing animals in the Cenozoic has contributed to the spread of grasses. Without large grazers, a clearcut of fire-destroyed area would soon be colonized by grasses and, if there is enough rain, tree seedlings. The tree seedlings would eventually produce shade, which kills most grasses. Large animals, however, trample the seedlings, killing the trees. Grasses persist because their lack of woody stems helps them to resist the damage of trampling.

Grass and Society

Grasses have long had significance in human society. They have been cultivated as a food source for domesticated animals for up to 10,000 years, and have been used to make paper since at least as early as 2400 B.C. Also, the primary ingredient of beer is usually barley or wheat, both grasses that have been used for this purpose for over 1000 years.

Some common aphorisms involve grass. For example:

- "The grass is always greener on the other side" suggests that an alternate state of affairs will always seem preferable to one's own.
- 'Don't let the grass grow under your feet' tells someone to get moving.
- 'A snake in the grass' means dangers that are hidden.
- "When elephants fight, it is the grass who suffers" tells of bystanders caught in the crossfire.

CHAPTER – 5

Ornamental Grass

Ornamental grasses are grasses grown as ornamental plants. They have become increasingly popular in gardens in recent years.

Along with true grasses (family Poaceae), the genus *Carex* (sedges) are often included in this classification. Their popularity relates both to their variety and to their three season contribution to the garden. Their long season is related to the lush new leaf growth in spring, and that the summer inflorescences (grass flowers and seed heads) are often dramatic and long lasting. Ornamental grasses can be brown, bluish, red, green, cream, and variegated.

Habits

Almost all ornamental grasses are perennials, coming up in spring, from their roots, which have stored large quantities of energy, and in fall or winter go dormant. Some, notably bamboos, are evergreen, and a few are annuals. Many are bunch grasses and tussock grasses. Sizes vary from a few centimetres up to several metres; the larger bamboos may reach 20 m or more tall. Some ornamental grasses are species that can be grown from seed. Many others are cultivars, and must be propagated by vegetative propagation of an existing plant.

Pampas Grass (*Cortaderia selloana*) is easily recognizable, with semi-dwarf to very large selections for the landscape. Deer Grass (*Muhlenbergia rigens*) and Canyon Prince Wild Blue Rye (*Leymus condensatus*) are popular in larger settings, natural landscaping, and native plant gardens. There are *Miscanthus* grasses whose variegations are horizontal, and appear even on a cloudy day to be stippled with sunshine. Many *Miscanthus* and *Pennisetum* species flower in mid or late summer, and the seed heads are long lasting, often remaining well into the winter. Some *Stipa* species flower in the spring, the inflorescence standing almost two metres above the clumps of leaves, and again the seed heads last late into the winter.

When gardening near natural wildland-urban interfaces, care to avoid invasive species, such as *Cortaderia jubata*, *Pennisetum setaceum*, and *Nassella tennuissima*, is responsible horticulture.

Examples

- *Festuca californica* (California Fescue)
- *Festuca idahoensis*
- *Muhlenbergia rigens* (Deer Grass)
- *Deschamsia cespitosa* (Tufted Hair-grass)
- *Calamagrostis foliosa* (Coastal or Leafy Reedgrass)
- *Panicum virgatum*
- *Melica imperfecta*
- *Agrostis nebulosa*
- *Leymus condensatus* (Canyon Prince Wild Blue Rye)
- *Helictotrichon sempervirens* (Blue Oat grass)
- *Pennisetum setaceum* var. *rubrum* (Red Fountain Grass)
- *Cortaderia selloana* (Pampas Grass)
- *Miscanthus sinensis*
- *Carex pansa* (Dune sedge)
- *Carex pendula* (Weeping sedge)

- *Carex praegracilis* (Field sedge)
- *Carex flacca* (C. glauca)
- *Carex spissa* (San Diego sedge)
- *Carex comans* and spp. and many cultivars (Japanese sedges)

Invasive Grasses

Grasses are one of the most abundant floras on all continents except Antarctica. Their divergence is estimated to have taken place 200 million years ago. Humans have intentionally and unintentionally introduced these species to North America through travel and trade. On the North American plains, prairies, grasslands, and meadows at least 11 per cent of grasses are non-native. North America is considered a hotspot for many invasive plant species of grasses, which threatens all of the endangered native grass species and potentially threatens other grass species. Conservation tactics and management policies can help prevent invasive species from taking over and driving native North American plants to extinction.

Non-native grasses are classified as invasive if they have the following three attributes:

1. The grass must have a pathway to be delivered to a new location, *e.g.* boat, shoe, animal, vehicle, feed, contaminated seed, etc.
2. It is able to tolerate its new environment long enough to establish and reproduce.
3. It is able to co-exist with native plants. Invasive grasses can outcompete native plants species by manipulating environmental conditions through either chemicals or other physiological factors.

These factors give an upper hand, which will allow the invader to outcompete the native plants. For example, a study conducted in the Mojave desert of California by Smith *et al.* in 2006, found that invasive grass species increase in areas with higher concentrations of carbon dioxide (CO_2), especially in arid conditions which make up 20 per cent of Earth's terrestrial surface area. Therefore, the annual invasive grasses will outcompete the natives because they use CO_2 to their advantage.

Impacts

There are many impacts involving invasive grasses in North America, which range from an ecosystem level to a community level to a genetic level. Such impacts influence habitat structure, disturbance regimes, and nutrient cycling. A successful invasion of a grass may result in new hybrid species, which can have both good and bad results. A good result could be a new species. A bad result could produce a sterile species, which would eventually lead to the extinction of that grass. European Cheatgrass invading the North American prairies is an example of a disturbance regime because it burns quickly and is very susceptible to fire. As a result, it gives invasive grasses a head start in the reproduction process. Another invasive grass impact example, at the ecological level, is Cordgrass or more specifically *Spartina anglica*. This species arose in England as an allotetraploid of two wild species and was introduced intentionally, to control erosion on the coasts of North America. It now flourishes spreading across the mudflats of the Pacific coast changing them into salt marshes, which has tremendous effects on the fauna of the mudflats such as clams, worms, and anemones.

Management

In order to keep North American native grasses from potentially going extinct from invasive grasses, it is important to control or better yet prevent such invasions in the first place. There are many ways to go about this such as controlling species mechanically or physically. This includes hand removal of grasses or by machine. In a five-year study conducted by Wilson *et al.* (2001) in Western Oregon, showed that mowing prairies of the invasive grass Arrhenatherum elatius allowed the native grasses Danthonia californica and

Festuca roemeri to flourish and out compete the non-natives. This is an effective method for the control of invasive grasses but it will take many hours of hard manual labor, which could be costly. Using chemicals is an effective way to control non-natives but it is not very ecologic friendly. Chemicals such as herbicides can contaminate waterways or kill other plants in the immediate area. Biological control is the use of other organism to reduce the invader grass. This has been proven to be effective but has also ricocheted back in a negative way. Other options include using multiple approaches at the same time, for example, mowing a specific region of grass land and then using an herbicide to target the invasive. The ultimate way to control invasive grasses in North America is to prevent them from entering in the first place. The first step of this prevention is identifying and regulating the grasses' pathway. After that it needs government assessment and policies to see that these pathways are blocked or regulated.

In this day and age it is almost impossible to prevent every non-native invasive grass into North America, but with the help of paid workers, volunteers, implementation plans, and tight regulations we will be able to control potential invaders. As for the invasive grasses that are already here, it is important to keep a strict control by implementing control strategies stated above. It is also important to use efficient yet effective methods to maintain a large biodiversity of flora.

CHAPTER – 6

Agrostis

Agrostis (bent or bentgrass) is a genus of over 100 species belonging to the grass family Poaceae.

Selected Species

- *Agrostis aequivalvi* (Arctic Bent)
- *Agrostis avenacea* (Pacific Bent)
- *Agrostis blasdalei* (Blasdale's Bent)
- *Agrostis canina* (Velvet Bent)
- *Agrostis capillaris* (Common Bent; Browntop) (= *A. tenuis*)
- *Agrostis castellana* (Highland Bent)
- *Agrostis clavata* (Northern Bent)
- *Agrostis curtisii* (Bristle Bent)
- *Agrostis densiflora* (California Bent)
- *Agrostis elliottiana* (Elliott's Bent)
- *Agrostis exarata* (Spike Bent)
- *Agrostis gigantea* (Black Bent; Redtop)
- *Agrostis goughensis*
- *Agrostis hallii* (Hall's Bent)

- *Agrostis hendersonii* (Henderson's Bent)
- *Agrostis hooveri* (Hoover's Bent)
- *Agrostis howellii* (Howell's Bent)
- *Agrostis hyemalis* (Winter Bent)
- *Agrostis idahoensis* (Idaho Bent)
- *Agrostis magellanica*
- *Agrostis mannii*
- *Agrostis media*
- *Agrostis mertensii* (Arctic Bent)
- *Agrostis microphylla* (Small-leaf Bent)
- *Agrostis oregonensis* (Oregon Bent)
- *Agrostis pallens* (Dune Bent, Seashore Bent)
- *Agrostis perennans* (Upland Bent)
- *Agrostis scabra* (Rough Bent, Tickle Bent)
- *Agrostis stolonifera* (Creeping Bent) (= *A. palustris*)
- *Agrostis tandilensis* (Kennedy's Bent)
- *Agrostis trachychlaena*
- *Agrostis variabilis* (Mountain Bent)
- *Agrostis vinealis* (Brown Bent)

Uses

Some species of bents are commonly used for lawn grass. This is a desirable grass for golf course tees, fairways and greens.

Bentgrass is used in turf applications for its numerous advantages: it can be mowed to a very short length without damage, it can handle a great amount of foot traffic, it has a shallow root system that is thick and dense allowing it to be seeded and grow rather easily, and it has a pleasing, deep green appearance. The name 'bent' refers to the shallow roots, which bend just below the surface of the soil to propagate laterally.

Creeping Bent

(*Agrostis stolonifera*) is the most commonly used species of *Agrostis*. Historically, it was often called Orcheston long grass, after a village on Salisbury Plain. It is cultivated almost exclusively on golf courses, especially on putting greens. Creeping Bent aggressively produces horizontal stems, called stolons, that run along the soil's surface. These allow Creeping Bent to form dense stands under conducive conditions and outcompete bunch-type grass and broadleaf weeds. As such, if infested in a home lawn, it can become a troublesome weed problem. The leaves of the bentgrass are long and slender.

Common Bent

(*Agrostis capillaris*) was brought to America from Europe. This was the type of grass that was used on the lawns of most estates. It is the tallest of the bents with very fine texture and like most bent grasses grows very dense. Although this species has been used on golf courses and sporting fields it is better suited for lawns. Colonial Bent is fairly easy to grow from seeds and fertilization of the lawn is not as intense. This grass also takes longer to establish than Creeping Bent. However it does not require the intense maintenance.

Velvet Bent

(*Agrostis canina*) gets it name for the velvet appearance that this grass produces. It has the finest texture of all the bent grasses. This grass was used in Europe for estate lawns and golf courses because it could be cut so short. This bent grass requires more upkeep and maintenance than Creeping Bent and because of this has been overlooked as a practical turf for current golf courses. This species also has a lighter colour than the two previous species.

Butterfly Foodplant

Butterflies whose caterpillars feed on *Agrostis* include:

- Zabulon Skipper, *Poanes zabulon*

Agrostis Stolonifera

Agrostis stolonifera (Creeping bentgrass, Creeping bent, Fiorin, Spreading bent, Carpet bentgrass, Redtop) is a perennial grass species in the Poaceae family. It is stoloniferous and may form mats or tufts. The prostrate stems of this species grow to 1.3-3.3 ft (0.4-1 m) long with 0.8-4in (2-10 cm) long leaf blades and a panicle reaching up to 16in (40 cm) in height. The ligule is pointed and up to 5mm long. This differs from Common Bent, Agrostis capillaris which is short and does not come to a point.

The leaves are tapering, often with a blue grey hue colour. The grass is not tufted and the spikelets are red and tightly closed within the panicle.

It flowers in July and August.

Distribution

It can be found growing in a variety of habitats including woodlands, grasslands and meadows, wetlands, riparian zones, and as a pioneer species on disturbed sites It is native to Eurasia and North Africa (Algeria, Morocco, and Tunisia). It is possible that it may also be to native to northern parts of North America, and in any case it has been widely introduced and naturalized on that continent and in many other places.

It is a constituent of wet habitats such as marshy grasslands. Some of its species have adapted to contaminated conditions and can cope with heavy metals. It can exist up to 2500 ft.

Cultivation

It is the most commonly used species of Agrostis.

The ability of creeping bentgrass to remain palatable and green in the summer is valued for livestock forage; it also provides good cover for upland game birds and waterfowl. It is used for turf in gardens and landscapes, particularly on golf courses.

CHAPTER – 7

Ammophila (Poaceae)

Ammophila (synonymous with *Psamma* P. Beauv.) is a genus consisting of two or three very similar species of grasses; common names for these grasses include Marram Grass, Bent Grass, and Beachgrass. These grasses are found almost exclusively on the first line of coastal sand dunes; their extensive systems of creeping underground stems or rhizomes allow them to thrive under conditions of shifting sands and high winds. *Ammophila* species are native to the coasts of the North Atlantic Ocean where they are usually the dominant species on sand dunes. Their native range includes few inland regions, with the Great Lakes of North America being the main exception. The genus name *Ammophila* (*Am-mó-phi-la*) originates from the Greek words of *Ammos*, meaning sand, and *Phillia*, meaning lover.

The *Ammophila* grasses are widely known as examples of xerophytes, which are plants that can withstand arid conditions such as deserts or sandy beaches. Its xerophytic adaptations (mentioned below) allow it to thrive under conditions most plants could not survive. Despite their occurrence on seacoasts, *Ammophila* grasses are not particularly tolerant of saline soils; they can tolerate a salinity of about 15 g/l (1.5%), which makes them 'moderate halophytes'.

Ammophila builds coastal sand dunes and thus stabilizes the sand. For this reason, the plants have been introduced far from their native range. Alfred Wiedemann writes that, starting in the early 19th century, *Ammophila arenaria* "has been introduced into virtually every British colonial settlement within its latitudinal tolerance range, including southeast and southwest Australia, New Zealand, South Africa, the Falkland Islands, and Norfolk Island. It has been planted widely in Japan and has been reported from Argentina and Chile." *Ammophila* species were introduced in the late 19th century on the Pacific coast of North America as well, and massive, intentional plantings were continued at least through 1960. In essentially all of the locations where they have been introduced, *Ammophila* plants are now listed as invasive, and costly efforts are underway to eradicate them.

Only two species seem incontrovertible:

1. *A. arenaria;* and
2. *A. breviligulata*

European Beachgrass

Native to coasts of Europe (north to Iceland) and northwest Africa. Inflorescence to 25 cm long; broad.

A. baltica has now been identified as a natural hybrid, ×*Ammocalamagrostis baltica*, between *Ammophila arenaria* and *Calamagrostis epigeios*. The hybrid occurs in parts of northern Europe, mainly from the Baltic Sea west to eastern England.

A. breviligulata—American Marram Grass or American Beachgrass. Native to coasts of eastern North America, including the shores of the Great Lakes. Inflorescence to 30 cm long; narrower than *A. arenaria*.

A. champlainensis or *A. breviligulata* ssp. *champlainensis*—Champlain Beachgrass. Native to shores of Lake Ontario and Lake Champlain. Inflorescence to 22 cm long; very similar to *A. breviligulata*, and no longer considered a distinct species by several authorities.

Ecology

In Europe, *Ammophila arenaria* has a coastal distribution, and is the dominant species on sand dunes where it is responsible for stabilising and building the foredune by capturing blown sand and binding it together with the warp and weft of its tough, fibrous rhizome system. Marram grass is strongly associated with two coastal plant community types in the British National Vegetation Classification. In community SD6 (Mobile dune) *Ammophila* is the dominant species. In the semi-fixed dunes (community SD7), where the quantity of blown sand is declining *Ammophila* becomes less competitive, and other species, notably *Festuca rubra* (Red Fescue) become prominent.

Uses

The ability of marram grass to grow on and bind sand makes it a useful plant in the stabilization of coastal dunes and artificial defences on sandy coasts. The usefulness was recognized in the late 18th century. On the North Sea coast of Jutland, Denmark, marram grass was traditionally much used for fuel, thatch, cattle fodder (after frost) etc. The use led to sand drift and loss of arable land. Hence, legislation promoting dune stabilization came into force in 1779 and 1792, successively leading to system of state-supported *dune planters* overlooked by *dune bailifs.* Marram grass was — and still is — propagated by root and shoot cuttings dug up locally and planted into the naked sand in periods of relatively calm and moist weather.

Newborough women once used marram grass in the manufacture of mats, haystack covers and brushes for whitewashing.

Marram grass has been widely used for thatch in many areas of the British isles close to the sea. The harvesting of marram grass for thatch was so widespread during the 17th century that it had the effect of destabilizing dunes, resulting in the burial of many villages, estates and farms. In 1695 the practice was banned by an Act of the Scottish Parliament.

Considering that many lands, meadowes and pasturages lying on sea coasts have been ruined and overspread in many places in this kingdom by sand driven from adjacent sand hills ... His Majesty does strictly prohibit and discharge the pulling of bent, broom or juniper off the sand hills for hereafter.

Eremochloa Ophiuroides

Centipede grass (*Eremochloa ophiuroides*) is a warm season lawn grass that is thick sod forming, uniform growing, and medium to light green colored. It has a coarse texture with short upright stems that grow to about 3-5 inches and spread by stolons.

Centipede has probably the lowest maintenance of the warm season grasses. It requires less mowing. Being a low growing grass, it has a much longer period of days between mowing cycles.

Centipede is rather drought-tolerant. Although the roots are not as deep as Bahia or Bermuda, its close to the ground growth allows for better conservation of water and helps fight drought.

It survives in mild cold temperatures as long as there aren't several hard freezes since it doesn't go into a true dormancy. With light freezes it will turn brown but recover and re-green as the temperature rises.

This creeping perennial is well adapted to low fertile sandy and acidic soils. The low fertilization requirement can be met by no more than a small summer application (with low phosphorus). Too much nitrogen encourages the stolons to grow above the soil instead of on the soil which then reduces its cold and drought tolerance.

When healthy, this full sun and slightly shade tolerant grass is aggressive enough to choke out weeds and other grasses.

Centipede seed is native to Southern China and was introduced to the United States in 1916. It has since become one of the most popular grasses in the south eastern states.

CHAPTER – 8

Bamboo

Bamboo is a group of perennial evergreens in the true grass family Poaceae, sub-family Bambusoideae, tribe Bambuseae. Giant bamboos are the largest members of the grass family. There are many types of bamboo, such as 'Fargesia Qinlingensis' in the Qinling Mountains in China.

In most bamboo, the internodal regions of the stem are hollow and the vascular bundles in the cross section are scattered throughout the stem instead of in a cylindrical arrangement. The dicotyledonous woody xylem is also absent. The absence of secondary growth wood causes the stems of monocots, even of palms and large bamboos, to be columnar rather than tapering.

Bamboos are some of the fastest growing plants in the world. They are capable of growing 100 cm (39 in.) or more per day due to a unique rhizome-dependent system. However, the growth rate is dependent on local soil and climatic conditions.

Bamboos are of notable economic and cultural significance in South Asia, South East Asia and East Asia, being used for building materials, as a food source, and as a versatile raw product.

In India, there is a debate over whether bamboo is a tree or a grass. Recently there was a controversy when the union ministry of environment and forests asked states across India to recognise bamboo as a minor forest produce.

There are more than 70 genera divided into about 1,450 species. Bamboo are found in diverse climates, from cold mountains to hot tropical regions. They occur across East Asia, from 50°N latitude in Sakhalin through to Northern Australia, and west to India and the Himalayas. They also occur in sub-Saharan Africa, and in the Americas from the Mid-Atlantic United States south to Argentina and Chile, reaching their southernmost point anywhere, at 47°S latitude. Continental Europe is not known to have any native species of bamboo.

There have recently been some attempts to grow bamboo on a commercial basis in the Great Lakes region of eastern-central Africa, especially in Rwanda.

Growth

Bamboo is one of the fastest-growing plants on Earth; it has been measured surging skyward as fast as 100 cm (39 in) in a 24-hour period. Primarily growing in regions of warmer climates during the Cretaceous period, vast fields existed in what is now Asia.

Unlike trees, all bamboo have the potential to grow to full height and girth in a single growing season of 3-4 months. During this first season, the clump of young shoots grow vertically, with no branching. In the next year, the pulpy wall of each culm or stem slowly dries and hardens. The culm begins to sprout branches and leaves from each node. During the third year, the culm further hardens. The shoot is now considered a fully mature culm. Over the next 2-5 years (depending on species), fungus and mould begin to form on the outside of the culm, which eventually penetrate and overcome the culm. Around 5-8 years later (species and climate dependent), the fungal and mold growth cause the culm to collapse and decay. This brief life means culms are ready for harvest and suitable for use in construction within about 3-7 years.

Although some bamboos flower every year, most species flower infrequently. In fact, many bamboos only flower at intervals as long as 60 or 120 years. These taxa exhibit mass flowering (or gregarious flowering), with all plants in the population flowering simultaneously. The longest mass flowering interval known is 130 years, and is found for all the species *Phyllostachys bambusoides* (Sieb. and Zucc.). In this species, all plants of the same stock flower at the same time, regardless of differences in geographic locations or climatic conditions, then the bamboo dies. The lack of environmental impact on the time of flowering indicates the presence of some sort of 'alarm clock' in each cell of the plant which signals the diversion of all energy to flower production and the cessation of vegetative growth. This mechanism, as well as the evolutionary cause behind it, is still largely a mystery.

One theory to explain the evolution of this semelparous mass flowering is the predator satiation hypothesis. This theory argues that by fruiting at the same time, a population increases the survival rate of their seeds by flooding the area with fruit so that even if predators eat their fill, there will still be seeds left over. By having a flowering cycle longer than the lifespan of the rodent predators, bamboos can regulate animal populations by causing starvation during the period between flowering events. Thus, according to this hypothesis, the death of the adult clone is due to resource exhaustion, as it would be more effective for parent plants to devote all resources to creating a large seed crop than to hold back energy for their own regeneration.

A second theory, the fire cycle hypothesis, argues that periodic flowering followed by death of the adult plants has evolved as a mechanism to create disturbance in the habitat, thus providing the seedlings with a gap in which to grow.

This hypothesis argues that the dead culms create a large fuel load, and also a large target for lightning strikes, increasing the likelihood of wildfire. Because bamboos are very aggressive as early successional plants, the seedlings would be able to outstrip other plants and take over the space left by their parents.

However, both have been disputed for different reasons. The predator satiation theory does not explain why the flowering cycle is 10 times longer than the lifespan of the local rodents, something not predicted by the theory. The bamboo fire cycle theory is considered by a few scientists to be unreasonable; they argue that fires only result from humans and there is no natural fire in India. This notion is considered wrong based on distribution of lightning strike data during the dry season throughout India. However, another argument against this theory is the lack of precedent for any living organism to harness something as unpredictable as lightning strikes to increase its chance of survival as part of natural evolutionary progress.

The mass fruiting also has direct economic and ecological consequences, however. The huge increase in available fruit in the forests often causes a boom in rodent populations, leading to increases in disease and famine in nearby human populations. For example, there are devastating consequences when the *Melocanna bambusoides* population flowers and fruits once every 30-35 years around the Bay of Bengal.

The death of the bamboo plants following their fruiting means the local people lose their building material, and the large increase in bamboo fruit leads to a rapid increase in rodent populations. As the number of rodents increase, they consume all available food, including grain fields and stored food, sometimes leading to famine. These rats can also carry dangerous diseases such as typhus, typhoid, and bubonic plague, which can reach epidemic proportions as the rodents increase in number.

Bamboo in Animal Diets

Soft bamboo shoots, stems, and leaves are the major food source of the Giant Panda of China, the Red Panda of Nepal and the Bamboo lemurs of Madagascar. Rats will eat the fruits as described above. Mountain Gorillas of Africa also feed on bamboo and have been documented consuming bamboo sap which was fermented and alcoholic; chimps and elephants of the region also eat the stalks.

Timber is harvested from cultivated and wild stands and some of the larger bamboos, particularly species in the genus *Phyllostachys*, are known as "timber bamboos".

Harvesting

Bamboo used for construction purposes must be harvested when the culms reach their greatest strength and when sugar levels in the sap are at their lowest, as high sugar content increases the ease and rate of pest infestation.

Harvesting of bamboo is typically undertaken according to the following cycles:

1. ***Life cycle of the clump:*** As each individual culm goes through a 5-7 year life cycle, culms are ideally allowed to reach this level of maturity prior to full capacity harvesting. The clearing out or thinning of culms, particularly older decaying culms, helps to ensure adequate light and resources for new growth. Well maintained clumps may have a productivity 3-4 times that of an unharvested wild clump.
2. ***Life cycle of the culm:*** As per the life cycle described above, bamboo is harvested from 2-3 years through to 5-7 years, depending on the species.
3. ***Annual cycle:*** As all growth of new bamboo occurs during the wet season, disturbing the clump during this phase will potentially damage the upcoming crop. Also during this high rain fall period, sap levels are at their highest and then diminish towards the dry season. Picking immediately prior to the wet/growth season may

also damage new shoots. Hence harvesting is best at the end of the dry season, a few months prior to the start of the wet.

4. ***Daily cycle:*** During the height of the day, Photosynthesis is at its peak producing the highest levels of sugar in sap, making this the least ideal time of day to harvest. Many traditional practitioners believe that the best time to harvest is at dawn or dusk on a full moon. This practice makes sense in terms of both moon cycles, visibility and daily cycles.

Leaching

Leaching is the removal of sap post-harvest. In many areas of the world the sap levels in harvested bamboo are reduced either through leaching or post-harvest photosynthesis.

Cut bamboo is raised clear of the ground and leant against the rest of the clump for 1-2 weeks until leaves turn yellow to allow full consumption of sugars by the plant.

A similar method is undertaken but with the base of the culm standing in fresh water, either in a large drum or stream to leach out sap.

Cut culms are immersed in a running stream and weighted down for 3-4 weeks.

Water is pumped through the freshly cut culms forcing out the sap (this method is often used in conjunction with the injection of some form of treatment).

In the process of water leaching, the bamboo is dried slowly and evenly in the shade to avoid cracking in the outer skin of the bamboo, thereby reducing opportunities for pest infestation.

Durability of bamboo in construction is directly related to how well it is handled from the moment of planting through harvesting, transportation, storage, design, construction and maintenance. Bamboo harvested at the correct time of year and then exposed to ground contact or rain, will break down just as quickly as incorrectly harvested material.

Ornamental Bamboos

There are two general patterns for the growth of bamboo: 'clumping' (sympodial) and 'running' (monopodial). Clumping bamboo species tend to spread slowly, as the growth pattern of the rhizomes is to simply expand the root mass gradually, similar to ornamental grasses. 'Running' bamboos, on the other hand, need to be taken care of in cultivation because of their potential for aggressive behaviour. They spread mainly through their roots and/or rhizomes, which can spread widely underground and send up new culms to break through the surface. Running bamboo species are highly variable in their tendency to spread; this is related to both the species and the soil and climate conditions. Some can send out runners of several metres a year, while others can stay in the same general area for long periods. If neglected, over time they can cause problems by moving into adjacent areas.

Bamboos seldom and unpredictably flower, and the frequency of flowering varies greatly from species to species. Once flowering takes place, a plant will decline and often die entirely. Although there are always a few species of bamboo in flower at any given time, collectors desiring to grow specific bamboo typically obtain their plants as divisions of already-growing plants, rather than waiting for seeds to be produced.

Regular maintenance will indicate major growth directions and locations. Once the rhizomes are cut, they are typically removed; however, rhizomes take a number of months to mature and an immature, severed rhizome will usually cease growing if left in-ground. If any bamboo shoots come up outside of the bamboo area afterwards, their presence indicates the precise location of the missed rhizome. The fibrous roots that radiate from the rhizomes do not produce more bamboo if they stay in the ground.

Bamboo growth can also be controlled by surrounding the plant or grove with a physical barrier. Typically, concrete and specially-rolled HDPE plastic are the materials used to create the barrier, which is placed in a 60-90 cm (2.0-3.0 ft) deep ditch around the planting, and angled out at the top to direct the rhizomes to the surface. (This is only possible if the barrier is installed in a straight line.) This method is very detrimental to ornamental bamboo as the bamboo within quickly becomes rootbound—showing all the signs of any unhealthy containerized plant. Symptoms include rhizomes escaping over the top, down underneath, and bursting the barrier. The bamboo within generally deteriorates in quality as fewer and fewer culms grow each year, culms live shorter periods, new culm diameter decreases, fewer leaves grow on the culms, and leaves turn yellow as the unnaturally contained rootmass quickly depletes the soil of nutrients, and curling leaves as the condensed roots cannot collect the water they need to sustain the foliage. Strong rhizomes and tools can penetrate plastic barriers with relative ease, so great care must be taken. Barriers usually fail sooner or later, or the bamboo within suffers greatly. Casual observation of many failed barriers has shown bursting of 60-mil (1.5 mm) HDPE in 5-6 years, and rhizomes diving underneath in as few as 3 years post install. In small areas regular maintenance is the only perfect method of controlling the spreading bamboos. Bamboo contained by barriers is much more difficult to remove than free-spreading bamboo. Barriers and edging are unnecessary for clump-forming bamboos. Clump-forming bamboos may eventually need to have portions removed if they become too large.

The ornamental plant sold in containers and marketed as 'lucky bamboo' is actually an entirely unrelated plant, *Dracaena sanderiana.* It is a resilient member of the lily family that grows in the dark, tropical rainforests of Southeast Asia and Africa. Lucky Bamboo has long been associated with the Eastern practice of Feng Shui. On a similar note, Japanese knotweed is also sometimes mistaken for a bamboo but it grows wild and is considered an invasive species.

The shoots (new bamboo culms that come out of the ground) of bamboo are edible. They are used in numerous Asian dishes and broths, and are available in supermarkets in various sliced forms, both fresh and canned version. The shoots of the giant bamboo (*Cathariostachys madagascariensis*) contain cyanide. Despite this, the Golden Bamboo Lemur ingests many times the quantity of toxin that would kill a human.

The bamboo shoot in its fermented state forms an important ingredient in cuisines across the Himalayas. In Assam, for example, it is called *khorisa*. In Nepal, a delicacy popular across ethnic boundaries consists of bamboo shoots fermented with turmeric and oil, and cooked with potatoes into a dish that usually accompanies rice (*alu tama* in Nepali).

In Indonesia, they are sliced thin and then boiled with *santan* (thick coconut milk) and spices to make a dish called *gulai rebung*. Other recipes using bamboo shoots are *Sayur Lodeh* (mixed vegetables in coconut milk) and *lun pia* (sometimes written *lumpia*: fried wrapped bamboo shoots with vegetables). The shoots of some species contain toxins that need to be leached or boiled out before they can be eaten safely.

Pickled bamboo, used as a condiment, may also be made from the pith of the young shoots.

The sap of young stalks tapped during the rainy season may be fermented to make *ulanzi* (a sweet wine) or simply made into a soft drink. Bamboo leaves are also used as wrappers for steamed dumplings which usually contains glutinous rice and other ingredients.

In Sambalpur, India, the tender shoots are grated into juliennes and fermented to prepare *kardi*. The name is derived from the Sanskrit word for bamboo shoot, 'karira'. This fermented bamboo shoot is used in various culinary preparations, notably 'amil', a sour vegetable soup. It is also made into pancakes using rice flour as a binding agent. The shoots that have turned a little fibrous are fermented, dried, and ground to sand sized particles to prepare a garnish known as 'hendua'. It is also cooked with tender pumpkin leaves to make sag green leaves.

The empty hollow in the stalks of larger bamboo is often used to cook food in many Asian cultures. Soups are boiled and rice is cooked in the hollows of fresh stalks of bamboo directly over a flame. Similarly, steamed tea is sometimes rammed into bamboo hollows to produce compressed forms of Pu-erh tea. Cooking food in bamboo is said to give the food a subtle but distinctive taste.

In addition, bamboo is frequently used for cooking utensils within many cultures and used in the manufacture of chopsticks. In modern times, some see bamboo tools as an eco-friendly alternative to other manufactured utensils.

Medicine

Bamboo is used in Chinese medicine for treating infections and healing.

It is a low-calorie source of potassium. It is known for its sweet taste and as a good source of nutrients and protein.

In Ayurveda, the Indian system of traditional medicine, the silicious concretion found in the culms of the bamboo stem is called *banslochan*. It is known as *tabashir* or *tawashir* in *Unani-Tibb* the Indo-Persian system of medicine. In English it is called 'bamboo manna'. This concretion is said to be a tonic for the respiratory diseases. It was earlier obtained from *Melocanna bambusoides* and is very hard to get. In most Indian literature, *Bambusa arundinacea* is described as the source of bamboo manna.

In its natural form, bamboo as a construction material is traditionally associated with the cultures of South Asia, East Asia and the South Pacific, to some extent in Central and South America and by extension in the aesthetic of Tiki culture. In China and India, bamboo was used to hold up simple suspension bridges, either by making cables of split bamboo or twisting whole culms of sufficiently pliable bamboo together. One such bridge in the area of Qian-Xian is referenced in writings dating back 960 A.D. and may have stood since as far back as the 3rd century B.C., due largely to continuous maintenance t has long been used as scaffolding; the practice has been banned in China for buildings over six stories but is still in continuous use for skyscrapers in Hong Kong. In the Philippines, the Nipa Hut is a fairly typical example of the most basic sort of housing that bamboo is used for; the walls are split and woven bamboo and bamboo slats and poles may be used as its support. In Japanese architecture, bamboo is used primarily as a supplemental and/or decorative element in buildings such as fencing, fountains, grates and gutters, largely due to the ready abundance of quality timber.

Various structural shapes may be made by training the bamboo to assume them as it grows. Squared sections of bamboo are created by compressing the growing stalk within a square form. Arches may similarly be created by forcing the bamboo's growth with the desired form and costs many times less than it would to assume the same shape in regular wood timber. More traditional forming methods such as the application of heat and pressure may also be used to curve or flatten the cut stalks.

Bamboo can be cut and laminated into sheets and planks. This process involves cutting stalks into thin strips, planing them flat, boiling and drying the strips which are then glued, pressed and finished. Generally long used in China and Japan, entrepreneurs started developing and selling laminated bamboo flooring in the West during the mid 1990s; products made from bamboo laminate including flooring, cabinetry, furniture and even decorative use are currently surging in popularity, transitioning from the boutique market to mainstream providers such as Home Depot. The bamboo goods industry (which also includes small goods, fabric, etc.) is expected to be worth $25 billion by the year 2012. The quality of bamboo laminate varies between manufacturers and the maturity of the plant from which it was harvested

(6 years being considered the optimum); the sturdiest products fulfill their claims of being up to three times harder than oak hardwood but others may be softer than standard hardwood.

Bamboo intended for use in construction should be treated to resist insects and rot. The most common solution for this purpose is a mixture of borax and boric acid. Another process involves boiling cut bamboo in order to remove the starches that attract bugs.

Bamboo has been used as reinforcement for concrete in those areas where it is plentiful, though dispute exists over its effectiveness in the various studies done on the subject. Bamboo does have the necessary strength to fulfil this function, but untreated bamboo will swell from the absorption of water from the concrete, causing it to crack. Several procedures must be followed to overcome this shortcoming.

Several institutes, businesses, and universities are working on the bamboo as an ecological construction material. In the United States and France, it is possible to get houses made entirely of bamboo, which are earthquake and cyclone-resistant and internationally certified. In Bali Indonesia there is an International primary school, named the Green School, which is constructed entirely of bamboo, due to its beauty, and advantages as a sustainable resource. There are three ISO standards for bamboo as a construction material.

In parts of India, bamboo is used for drying clothes indoors, both as the rod high up near the ceiling to hang clothes on as well as the stick that is wielded with acquired expert skill to hoist, spread, and to take down the clothes when dry. It is also commonly used to make ladders, which apart from their normal function are also used for carrying bodies in funerals. In Maharashtra the bamboo groves and forests are called VeLuvana, the name VeLu for Bamboo most likely from Sanskrit, while Vana is forest.

Furthermore, bamboo is also used to create flagpoles for saffron coloured, Hindu religious flags, which can be seen fluttering across India, especially Bihar and Uttar Pradesh, as well as in Guyana and Suriname.

Furniture

Bamboo has a long history of use in Asian furniture. Chinese bamboo furniture is a distinct style based on millennia-long tradition.

Textiles

Because the fibres of bamboo are very short (less than 3mm), they are impossible to transform into yarn in a natural process. The usual process by which textiles labeled as being made of bamboo are produced uses only the rayon, that is being made out of the fibers with heavy employment of chemicals. To accomplish this, the fibers are broken down with chemicals and extruded through mechanical spinnerets; the chemicals include lye, carbon disulfide and strong acids. Retailers have sold both end products as 'bamboo fabric' to cash in on bamboo's current eco-friendly cachet, however the Canadian Competition Bureau and the US Federal Trade Commission, as of mid-2009, are cracking down on the practice of labeling bamboo rayon as natural bamboo fabric. Under the guidelines of both agencies these products must be labeled as rayon with the optional qualifier 'from bamboo'. Bamboo fabric is known for its softness and boasts strong absorbency and anti-microbial properties, though the chemical process in bamboo rayon destroys any anti-microbial quality.

A new bamboo fabric has been developed at Beijing University and has created an interest in bamboo clothing, particularly those interested in using organic material. Clothing from bamboo is soft and comparable to cashmere.

Bamboo has natural antibacterial and antifungal qualities that help the plant fight off disease and insects. These properties come from a naturally occurring substance in bamboo called kun. Because these qualities are not lost during processing or washing, bamboo fabrics are able to retain these qualities and do not hold odors like some fabrics do.

Paper

Bamboo fibre has been used to make paper in China since early times. A high quality hand-made paper is still produced in small quantities. Coarse bamboo paper is still used to make spirit money in many Chinese communities.

Bamboo pulps are maninly produced in China, Myanmar, Thailand and India and are used in printing and writing papers . The most common bamboo species used for paper are *Dendrocalamus asper* and *Bamboo bluemanea.* It is also possible to make dissolving pulp from bamboo. The average fibre length is similar to hardwoods, but the properties of bamboo pulp are closer to softwoods pulps due to it have a very broad fibre length distribution.

Musical Instruments

Bamboo's natural hollow form makes it an obvious choice for many instruments, particularly wind and percussion. There are numerous types of bamboo flute made all over the world, such as the dizi, xiao, shakuhachi, palendag, jinghu. In India it is a very popular and highly respected musical instrument, available even to the poorest and the choice of many highly venerated maestros of classical music. It is known and revered above all as the divine flute forever associated with Lord Krishna, who is always portrayed holding a bansuri in sculptures and paintings. Four of the instruments used in Polynesia for traditional hula are made of bamboo: nose flute, rattle, stamping pipes and the Jew's harp. Bamboo may be used in the construction of the Australian didgeridoo instead of the more traditional eucalyptus wood. In Indonesia and the Philippines, bamboo has been used for making various kinds of musical instruments including the kolintang, angklung, and bumbong. Traditional Philippine 'banda kawayan' (bamboo bands) use a variety of bamboo musical instruments including the marimba, angklung, panpipes, bumbong, as well as bamboo versions of western instruments such as clarinets, saxophones, and tubas. The Las Piñas Bamboo Organ in the Philippines has pipes made of bamboo culms. The modern amplified string instrument the Chapman Stick is also constructed using bamboo. The khene (also spelled 'khaen', 'kaen' and 'khen'; Lao) is a mouth organ of Lao origin whose pipes, which are usually made of bamboo, are connected with a small, hollowed-out hardwood reservoir into which air is blown, creating a sound similar to that of the violin. In the Indian Ocean island of Madagascar, the *valiha*, a long tube zither made of a single bamboo stalk, is considered the national instrument.

Water Processing

Bamboo as a versatile material is demonstrated by its use in water desalination. A Bamboo filter is used to remove the salt from saltwater.

Transportation

Several manufacturers offer bamboo bicycles.

Landscaping

Bamboo is widely used in landscaping due to its ability to grow quickly in thick, tall sections. It makes an excellent privacy barrier, while also providing a nice aesthetic.

Angling

Due to its flexibility bamboo is also used to make fishing rods. The split cane rod is especially prized for fly fishing.

Bamboo's long life makes it a Chinese symbol of longevity, while in India it is a symbol of friendship. The rarity of its blossoming has led to the flowers' being regarded as a sign of impending famine. This may be due to rats feeding upon the profusion of flowers, then multiplying and destroying a large part of the local food supply. The most recent flowering began in May 2006 . Bamboo is said to bloom in this manner only about every 50 years.

In Chinese culture, the bamboo, plum blossom, orchid, and chrysanthemum are collectively referred to as the Four Gentlemen. These four plants also represent the four seasons and, in Confucian ideology, four aspects of the *junzi* ('prince' or 'noble one').

The pine tree, the bamboo, and the plum blossom are also admired for their perseverance under harsh conditions, and are together known as the 'Three Friends in Winter'. The 'Three Friends' is traditionally used as a system of ranking in Japan, for example in sushi sets or accommodations at a traditional Ryokan (inn). Pine is of the first rank, bamboo (*také* ?) is of second rank, and plum (*ume* ?) is of the third.

In Japan, a bamboo forest sometimes surrounds a Shinto shrine as part of a sacred barrier against evil. Many Buddhist temples also have bamboo groves.

In northern Indian state of Assam, the fermented bamboo paste known as khorisa is known locally as a folk remedy for the treatment of impotence, infertility, and menstrual pains.

A cylindrical bamboo brush holder or holder of poems on scrolls, created by Zhang Xihuang in the 17th century, late Ming or early Qing Dynasty. In the calligraphy of Zhang's style, the poem *Returning to My Farm in the Field* by the 4th century poet Tao Yuanming is incised on the holder.

Bamboo plays an important part of the culture of Vietnam. Bamboo symbolizes the spirit of Vovinam (a Vietnamese martial arts): "cuong nhu ph?i tri?n" (coordination between hard and soft (martial arts)). Bamboo also symbolizes the Vietnamese hometown and Vietnamese soul: the gentlemanlike, straightforwardness, hard working, optimism, unity and adaptableness. A Vietnamese proverb says: "When the bamboo is old, the bamboo sprouts appear", the meaning being Vietnam will never be annihilated; if the previous generation dies, the children take their place.

Therefore the Vietnam nation and Vietnamese value will be maintained and developed eternally. Traditional Vietnamese villages are surrounded by thick bamboo hedges (*luy tre*).

The Song Dynasty (960-1279 AD) Chinese scientist and polymath Shen Kuo (1031-1095) used the evidence of underground petrified bamboo found in the dry northern climate of Yan'an, Shanbei region, Shaanxi province to support his geological theory of gradual climate change.

Other Cultures

The ethnic group known as the Bozo of West Africa, take their name from the Bambara phrase *bo-so*, which means 'bamboo house'.

The bamboo is the national plant of St. Lucia.

Myths and Legends

Several Asian cultures, including that of the Andaman Islands, believe that humanity emerged from a bamboo stem. In the Philippine creation myth, legend tells that the first man and the first woman each emerged from split bamboo stems on an island created after the battle of the elemental forces (Sky and Ocean). In Malaysian legends a similar story includes a man who dreams of a beautiful woman while sleeping under a bamboo plant; he wakes up and breaks the bamboo stem, discovering the woman inside. The Japanese folktale 'Tale of the Bamboo Cutter' (*Taketori Monogatari*) tells of a princess from the Moon emerging from a shining bamboo section. Hawaiian bamboo ('ohe) is a kinolau or body form of the Polynesian creator god Kane.

Bamboo cane is also the weapon of Vietnamese legendary hero Saint Giong- who had grown up immediately and magically since the age of 3 years old because of his national liberating wish against Ân invaders.

An ancient Vietnamese legend (The Hundred-knot Bamboo Tree) tells of a poor, young farmer who fell in love with his landlord's beautiful daughter. The farmer asked the landlord for his daughter's hand in marriage, but the proud landlord would not allow her to be bound in marriage to a poor farmer. The landlord decided to foil the marriage with an impossible deal; the farmer must bring him a 'bamboo tree of one-hundred nodes'. But Buddha (*B?t*) appeared to the farmer and told him that such a tree could be made from one-hundred nodes from several different trees. *B?t* gave to him four magic words to attach the many nodes of bamboo: which means "joined together immediately, fell apart immediately". The triumphant farmer returned to the landlord and demanded his daughter. Curious to see such a long bamboo, the landlord was magically joined to the bamboo when he touched it as the young farmer said the first two magic words. The story ends with the happy marriage of the farmer and the landlord's daughter after the landlord agreed to the marriage and asked to be separated from the bamboo.

In China, there is a legend that the Emperor Yao gave two of his daughters as a test for his potential to rule to the future Emperor Shun. Shun passed the test of being able to run his household with the two emperor's daughters as wives, and thus Yao made Shun his successors, bypassing his unworthy son. Later Shun drowned in the Xiang River. The tears that his two bereaved wives let fall upon the bamboos growing there explains the origin of spotted bamboo. The two women later became goddesses.

Bamboo as a Writing Surface

Bamboo was in widespread use in early China as a medium for written documents. The earliest surviving examples of such documents, written in ink on string-bound bundles of bamboo strips (or 'slips'), date from the 5th c. BC during the Warring States period. However, references in earlier texts surviving on other media make it clear that some precursor of these Warring States period bamboo slips was in use as early as the late Shang period (from about 1250 BC).

Bamboo or wooden strips were the standard writing material during the Han dynasty and excavated examples have been found in abundance. Subsequently, paper began to displace bamboo and wooden strips from mainstream uses, and by the 4th C. AD bamboo had been largely abandoned as a medium for writing in China. Several paper industries are surviving on Bamboo forests. Ballarpur (Chandrapur, Maharstra) paper mills uses bamboo for paper production.

Bamboo as a Weapon

Bamboo is used in several East Asian and South Asian martial arts.

In the ancient Tamil martial art of Silambam, fighters would hit each other rapidly with bamboo sticks.

In the Japanese martial art Kendo, bamboo is used to make the Shinai sword.

A bamboo stick can be made into a simple spear by sharpening one of the ends.

Archery longbow and recurve bow limbs are commonly crafted with flat ground bamboo, and make superior weapons for bowhunting and target archery.

CHAPTER – 9

Ryegrass

Ryegrass (*Lolium*) is a genus of nine species of tufted grasses in the Pooideae subfamily of the Poaceae family. Also called tares (even though there is no firm evidence that this is the same as the plant given that name in English language translations of the Bible — vetches are another candidate), these plants are native to Europe, Asia and northern Africa, but are widely cultivated and naturalized elsewhere. Ryegrasses are naturally diploid, with 2n = 14, and are closely related to the fescues *festuca*.

Ryegrass should not be confused with rye, which is a grain crop.

The following are accepted as distinct species:

- *Lolium canariense* Steud—Canary Islands Ryegrass
- *Lolium edwardii* H.Scholz, Stierst and Gaisberg
- *Lolium multiflorum* Lam—Italian Ryegrass
- *Lolium perenne* L.—Perennial Ryegrass
- *Lolium persicum*—Persian Ryegrass or Persian Darnel
- *Lolium remotum* Schrank
- *Lolium rigidum* Gaudin—Stiff Darnel, Wimmera Ryegrass
- *Lolium temulentum* L.—Darnel, Poison Darnel

Cultivation and Uses

Ryegrasses contain some species which are important grasses for both lawns, and as pasture and for grazing and hay for livestock, being a highly nutritious stock feed. Ryegrasses are also used in soil erosion control programmes. It is the principal grazing grass in New Zealand where some 10 million kilograms of certified seed are produced every year. There is a large range of cultivars. The primary species found worldwide and used for both lawns and as a forage crop is perennial ryegrass (*Lolium perenne*). Like many cool-season grasses, it is often infected by a clandestine, fungal endophyte which lives symbiotically within its leaves.

Some species, particularly *L. temulentum*, are weeds which can have a severe impact on the production of wheat and other crops. Ryegrass pollen is also one of the major causes of hay fever.

Many grass tennis courts are also made of rye grass in different compositions depending on the tournament.

Synonyms

- *Lolium temulentum* (Poison Darnel)
- *L. ambiguum* = Lolium multiflorum
- *L. annuum* = *Lolium temulentum*
- *L. arundinaceum* = *Festuca arundinacea*
- *L. berteronianum* = *Lolium temulentum*
- *L. brasilianum* = *Lolium perenne*
- *L. canadense* = *Lolium perenne*
- *L. crassiculme* = *Lolium rigidum*
- *L. cuneatum* = *Lolium temulentum*
- *L. dorei* = *Lolium persicum*
- *L. giganteum* = *Festuca gigantea*
- *L. gracile* = *Lolium temulentum*
- *L. lepturoides* = *Lolium rigidum* subsp. *lepturoides*

- *L. marschallii* = *Lolium perenne*
- *L. parabolicae* = *Lolium rigidum*
- *L. pratense* = *Festuca pratensis*
- *L. remotum* = *Lolium temulentum* subsp. *remotum*
- *L. romanum* = *Lolium multiflorum*
- *L. scabrum* = *Lolium multiflorum*
- *L. siculum* = *Lolium multiflorum*
- *L. subulatum* = *Lolium rigidum* subsp. *lepturoides*
- *L. teres* = *Lolium rigidum* subsp. *lepturoides*
- *L. trabutii* = *Lolium rigidum*

Festuca

Festuce (*Festuca*) is a genus of about 300 species of perennial tufted grasses, belonging to the grass family Poaceae (subfamily Pooideae). The genus has a cosmopolitan distribution, although the majority of the species are found in cool temperate areas, such as the transition zone and Canada. The genus is closely related to ryegrass (*Lolium*), and recent evidence from phylogenetic studies using DNA sequencing of plant mitochondrial DNA shows that the genus lacks monophyly. As a result plant taxonomists have placed several species, including the forage grasses, tall fescue and meadow fescue, formerly belonging to the genus *Festuca* into the genus *Lolium*.

Fescues range from small grasses only 10 cm tall or less with very fine thread-like leaves less than 1 mm wide, to tall grasses up to 2 m tall with large leaves up to 60 cm (2 ft) long and 2 cm (3/4 in.) broad.

Fescue pollen is a significant contributor to hay fever.

The fescues contain some species which are important grasses for both lawns (particularly the fine-leaved species, highly valued for bowling greens) and as pasture and hay for livestock, being a highly nutritious stock feed. Fescues are also quite common on golf courses of the coastal U.S. and the U.K., usually beyond the second cut in the rough.

They are also used in soil erosion control programmes, most notably tall fescue, one cultivar of which, Kentucky 31 (*Festuca arundinacea*), was used in land reclamation during the dust bowl period in the 1930s in the US.

Fescue is sometimes used as feed for horses. However, fescue poisoning, which results from ergot alkaloids produced by an endophytic fungus, is a risk for pregnant mares. Occurring in the last three months of pregnancy, fescue poisoning increases the risk of spontaneous abortion, stillbirths, retained placenta, absent milk production, and prolonged pregnancy. Fescue Toxicosis of livestock can require a farmer to seek costly treatment for his animals. Incorporating legumes into the fescue can be a way to increase livestock gains and conception rates, even if the fescue is infected.

Selected Species

- *Festuca altaica*—Northern Rough Fescue
- *Festuca alpina*—Alpine Fescue
- *Festuca altissima*—Wood Fescue
- *Festuca amethystina*—Tufted Fescue
- *Festuca amplissima*
- *Festuca arizonica*—Arizona Fescue
- *Festuca arvernensis*
- *Festuca caesia*—Blue Fescue
- *Festuca californica*—California Fescue
- *Festuca cinerea*—Elijah Blue Fescue
- *Festuca contracta*—Tufted Fescue
- *Festuca diffusa*—Northern Fescue
- *Festuca donax*
- *Festuca elegans*
- *Festuca elmeri*—Coast Fescue
- *Festuca eskia*

- *Festuca gautieri*
- *Festuca glacialis*
- *Festuca glauca*—Grey Fescue
- *Festuca heterophylla*—Various-leaved Fescue
- *Festuca hallii*—Plains Rough Fescue
- *Festuca idahoensis*—Idaho Fescue
- *Festuca jubata*
- *Festuca juncifolia*—Rush-leaved Fescue
- *Festuca mairei*—Atlas Fescue
- *Festuca matthewsii*—Alpine Fescue Tussock
- *Festuca nigrescens*—Alpine Chewing's Fescue
- *Festuca novae-zealandiae*—Fescue Tussock
- *Festuca occidentalis*—Western Fescue
- *Festuca ovina*—Sheep's Fescue
- *Festuca paniculata*—East Alpine Violet Fescue
- *Festuca picturata*
- *Festuca pilgeri*
- *Festuca polesica*
- *Festuca pseudodura*
- *Festuca punctoria*
- *Festuca pyrenaica*
- *Festuca quadriflora*
- *Festuca richardsonii*—Arctic Fescue
- *Festuca rubra*—Red Fescue
- *Festuca rubra* subsp. *commutata* Chewing's Fescue
- *Festuca rupicola*
- *Festuca sativa*
- *Festuca scabrella*—Rough Fescue
- *Festuca subulata*—Bearded Fescue
- *Festuca subulifolia*—Crinkleawn Fescue

- *Festuca supina*—Tufted Fescue
- *Festuca tenuifolia*—Fine-leaved Sheep's Fescue
- *Festuca viridula*—Green Fescue
- *Festuca vivipara*—Viviparous Fescue
- Subgenus *Schedonorus*, proposed for inclusion in genus *Lolium*
- *Festuca arundinacea* (syn. *Festuca elatior*, *Lolium arundinaceum*)—Tall Fescue
- *Festuca gigantea* (*Lolium giganteum*)—Giant Fescue
- *Festuca mazzettiana* (*Lolium mazzettianum*)
- *Festuca pratensis* (*Lolium pratensis*)—Meadow Fescue

CHAPTER – 10

Sugarcane

Sugarcane refers to any of 6 to 37 species (depending on which taxonomic system is used) of tall perennial grasses of the genus *Saccharum* (family Poaceae, tribe Andropogoneae). Native to warm temperate to tropical regions of Asia, they have stout, jointed, fibrous stalks that are rich in sugar, and measure two to six metres (six to nineteen feet) tall. All sugar cane species interbreed, and the major commercial cultivars are complex hybrids.

Sugar cane products include table sugar, falernum, molasses, rum, *cachaça* (the national spirit of Brazil), bagasse and ethanol.

Sugarcane is indigenous to tropical South Asia and Southeast Asia. Different species likely originated in different locations, with *S. barberi* originating in India and *S. edule* and *S. officinarum* coming from New Guinea. Crystallized sugar was reported 5,000 years ago in the Indus Valley Civilization, located in modern-day Pakistan and northwest India.

Around the eighth century A.D., Muslim traders introduced sugar from South Asia to the other parts of the Islamic empire in Mediterranean, Mesopotamia, Egypt,

North Africa, and Andalusia. By the tenth century, sources state, there was no village in Mesopotamia that did not grow sugar cane. It was among the early crops brought to the Americas by the Andalusians (from their fields in the Canary Islands), and the Portuguese.

'Boiling houses' in the 17th through 19th centuries converted sugarcane juice into raw sugar. These houses were attached to sugar plantations in the western colonies. Slaves often ran the boiling process, under very poor conditions. Made of cut stone, rectangular boxes of brick or stone served as furnaces with an opening at the bottom to stoke the fire and remove ashes. At the top of each furnace were up to seven copper kettles or boilers, each one smaller and hotter than the previous one. The cane juice began in the largest kettle. The juice was then heated and lime added to remove impurities. The juice was skimmed, then channelled to successively smaller kettles. The last kettle, which was called the 'teache', was where the cane juice became syrup. The next step was a cooling trough, where the sugar crystals hardened around a sticky core of molasses. This raw sugar was then shovelled from the cooling trough into hogsheads (wooden barrels), and from there into the curing house.

Sugarcane is still extensively grown in the Caribbean. Christopher Columbus first brought it during his second voyage to the Americas, initially to the island of Hispaniola (modern day Haiti and the Dominican Republic). In colonial times, sugar formed one side of the triangular trade of New World raw materials, European manufactures, and African slaves.

France found its sugarcane islands so valuable, it effectively traded its portion of Canada, famously dubbed 'a few acres of snow', to Britain for their return of Guadeloupe, Martinique and St. Lucia at the end of the Seven Years' War. The Dutch similarly kept Suriname, a sugar colony in South America, instead of seeking the return of the New Netherlands (New York).

Cuban sugarcane produced sugar that received price supports from and a guaranteed market in the USSR; the dissolution of that country forced the closure of most of Cuba's sugar industry. Sugarcane remains an important part of the economy of Guyana, Belize, Barbados and Haiti, along with the Dominican Republic, Guadeloupe, Jamaica, and other islands.

Sugarcane production greatly influenced many tropical Pacific Islands, including Okinawa and, most particularly, Hawai i and Fiji. In these islands, sugarcane came to dominate the economic and political landscape after the arrival of powerful European and American agricultural businesses, which promoted immigration of workers from various Asian countries to tend and harvest the crop. Sugar was the dominant factor in diversifying the islands' ethnic make-up, profoundly affecting their politics and society.

Brazil is the biggest grower of sugarcane, which goes for sugar and ethanol for gasoline-ethanol blends (gasohol) for transportation fuel. In India, sugarcane is sold as jaggery, and also refined into sugar, primarily for consumption in tea and sweets, and for the production of alcoholic beverages.

Today, sugarcane is grown in over 110 countries. In 2009, an estimated 1,683 million metric tons were produced worldwide which amounts to 22.4 per cent of the total world agricultural production by weight. About 50 per cent of production occurs in Brazil and India.

Sugarcane cultivation requires a tropical or temperate climate, with a minimum of 60 centimetres (24 in) of annual moisture. It is one of the most efficient photosynthesizers in the plant kingdom. It is a C_4 plant, able to convert up to one per cent of incident solar energy into biomass. In prime growing regions, such as India, Pakistan, Peru, Brazil, Bolivia, Colombia, Australia, Ecuador, Cuba, the Philippines, El Salvador and Hawaii, sugarcane can produce 20 lb (9 kg) for each square metre exposed to the sun.

Although sugarcanes produce seeds, modern stem cutting has become the most common reproduction method. Each cutting must contain at least one bud and the cuttings are sometimes hand-planted. In more technologically advanced countries like the United States and Australia, billet planting is common. Billets harvested from a mechanical harvester are planted by a machine which opens and recloses the ground.

Once planted, a stand can be harvested several times; after each harvest, the cane sends up new stalks, called ratoons. Successive harvests give decreasing yields, eventually justifying replanting. Two to ten harvests may be possible between plantings.

Sugarcane is harvested by hand and mechanically. Hand harvesting accounts for more than half of production, and is dominant in the developing world. In hand harvesting, the field is first set on fire. The fire burns dry leaves, and kills any lurking venomous snakes, without harming the stalks and roots. Harvesters then cut the cane just above ground-level using cane knives or machetes. A skilled harvester can cut 500 kilograms (1,100 lb) of sugarcane per hour.

Mechanical harvesting uses a combine, or chopper harvester. The Austoft 7000 series, the original modern harvester design, has now been copied by other companies, including Cameco/John Deere. The machine cuts the cane at the base of the stalk, strips the leaves, chops the cane into consistent lengths and deposits the cane into a transporter following alongside.

The harvester then blows the trash back onto the field. Such machines can harvest 100 long tons (100 t) each hour; however, harvested cane must be rapidly processed. Once cut, sugarcane begins to lose its sugar content, and damage to the cane during mechanical harvesting accelerates this decline. This decline is offset by the fact that a modern chopper harvester can complete the harvest faster and more efficiently than hand cutting and loading.

Austoft also developed a series of hydraulic high-lift infield transporters to work alongside their harvesters to allow even more rapid transfer of cane to, for example, the nearest railway siding.

Pests

The cane beetle (also known as cane grub) can substantially reduce crop yield by eating roots; it can be controlled with imidacloprid (Confidor) or chlorpyrifos (Lorsban). Other important pests are the larvae of some butterfly/moth species, including the turnip moth, the sugarcane borer (*Diatraea saccharalis*), the Mexican rice borer (*Eoreuma loftini*); leaf-cutting ants, termites, spittlebugs (especially *Mahanarva fimbriolata* and *Deois flavopicta*), and the beetle *Migdolus fryanus*. The planthopper insect *Eumetopina flavipes* acts as a virus vector, which causes the sugarcane disease ramu stunt.

Numerous pathogens infect sugarcane, such as sugarcane grassy shoot disease caused by *Phytoplasma*, whiptail disease or sugarcane smut, *pokkah boeng* caused by *Fusarium moniliforme*, and red rot disease caused by *Colletotrichum falcatum*. Viral diseases affecting sugarcane include sugarcane mosaic virus, maize streak virus, and sugarcane yellow leaf virus. See the list of sugarcane diseases.

Nitrogen Fixation

Some sugarcane varieties are known to be capable of fixing atmospheric nitrogen in association with the bacterium *Glucoacetobacter diazotrophicus*. Unlike legumes and other nitrogen fixing plants which form root nodules in the soil in association with bacteria, *G. diazotrophicus* lives within the intercellular spaces of the sugarcane's stem.

Traditionally, sugarcane processing requires two stages. Mills extract raw sugar from freshly harvested cane, and sometimes bleach it to make 'mill white' sugar for local consumption. Refineries, often located nearer to consumers in North America, Europe, and Japan, then produce refined white sugar, which is 99 per cent sucrose. These two stages are slowly merging. Increasing affluence in the sugar-producing tropics increased demand for refined sugar products, driving a trend toward combined milling and refining.

Refining

Sugar refining further purifies the raw sugar. It is first mixed with heavy syrup and then centrifuged in a process called 'affination'. Its purpose is to wash away the sugar crystals' outer coating, which is less pure than the crystal interior. The remaining sugar is then dissolved to make a syrup, about 60 per cent solids by weight.

The sugar solution is clarified by the addition of phosphoric acid and calcium hydroxide, which combine to precipitate calcium phosphate. The calcium phosphate particles entrap some impurities and absorb others, and then float to the top of the tank, where they can be skimmed off. An alternative to this 'phosphatation' technique is 'carbonatation,' which is similar, but uses carbon dioxide and calcium hydroxide to produce a calcium carbonate precipitate.

After filtering any remaining solids, the clarified syrup is decolorized by filtration through activated carbon. Bone char is traditionally used in this role. Some remaining colour-forming impurities adsorb to the carbon.

The purified syrup is then concentrated to supersaturation and repeatedly crystallized in a vacuum, to produce white refined sugar. As in a sugar mill, the sugar crystals are separated from the molasses by centrifuging. Additional sugar is recovered by blending the remaining syrup with the washings from affination and again crystallizing to produce brown sugar. When no more sugar can be economically recovered, the final molasses still contains 20-30 per cent sucrose and 15-25 per cent glucose and fructose.

To produce granulated sugar, in which individual grains do not clump, sugar must be dried, first by heating in a rotary dryer, and then by blowing cool air through it for several days.

Ribbon Cane Syrup

Ribbon cane is a subtropical type that was once widely grown in the southern United States, as far north as coastal North Carolina. The juice was extracted with horse or mule-powered crushers; the juice was boiled, like maple syrup, in a flat pan, and then used in the syrup form as a food sweetener. It is not currently a commercial crop, but a few growers find ready sales for their product.

In India, the states of Uttar Pradesh (38.57%), Maharashtra (17.76%) and Karnataka (12.20%) lead the nation in sugarcane production.

In the United States, sugar cane is grown commercially in Florida, Hawaii, Louisiana, and Texas.

Cane Ethanol

Ethanol is generally available as a byproduct of sugar production. It can be used as a biofuel alternative to gasoline, and is widely used in cars in Brazil. It is an alternative to gasoline, and may become the primary product of sugarcane processing, rather than sugar.

At present, 75 tons of raw sugarcane are produced annually per hectare in Brazil. The cane delivered to the processing plant is called burned and cropped (b&c), and represents 77 per cent of the mass of the raw cane. The reason for this reduction is that the stalks are separated from the leaves (which are burned and whose ashes are left in the field as fertilizer), and from the roots that remain in the ground to sprout for the next crop. Average cane production is, therefore, 58 tons of b&c per hectare per year.

Each ton of b&c yields 740 kg of juice (135 kg of sucrose and 605 kg of water) and 260 kg of moist bagasse (130 kg of dry bagasse). Since the higher heating value of sucrose is

16.5 MJ/kg, and that of the bagasse is 19.2 MJ/kg, the total heating value of a ton of b&c is 4.7 GJ of which 2.2 GJ come from the sucrose and 2.5 from the bagasse.

Per hectare per year, the biomass produced corresponds to 0.27 TJ. This is equivalent to 0.86 W per square meter. Assuming an average insolation of 225 W per square meter, the photosynthetic efficiency of sugar cane is 0.38 per cent.

The 135 kg of sucrose found in 1 ton of b&c are transformed into 70 litres of ethanol with a combustion energy of 1.7 GJ. The practical sucrose-ethanol conversion efficiency is, therefore, 76 per cent (compare with the theoretical 97 per cent).

One hectare of sugar cane yields 4,000 litres of ethanol per year (without any additional energy input, because the bagasse produced exceeds the amount needed to distill the final product). This, however, does not include the energy used in tilling, transportation, and so on. Thus, the solar energy-to-ethanol conversion efficiency is 0.13 per cent.

Sugarcane as Food

In most countries where sugarcane is cultivated, there are several foods and popular dishes derived directly from it, such as:

- *Raw sugarcane:* chewed to extract the juice;
- *Sugarcane juice:* a combination of fresh juice, extracted by hand or small mills, with a touch of lemon and ice to make a popular drink, known variously as *usacha rass, guarab, guarapa, guarapo, papelón, aseer asab, ganna sharbat, mosto, caldo de cana*;
- *Cachaça:* the most popular distilled alcoholic beverage in Brazil; a liquor made of the distillation of sugarcane; and
- *Jaggery:* a solidified molasses, known as *gur* or *gud* in India, traditionally produced by evaporating juice to make a thick sludge, and then cooling and molding it in buckets.

Modern production partially freeze dries the juice to reduce caramelization and lighten its colour. It is used as sweetener in cooking traditional entrees, sweets and desserts.

- *Panela*: solid pieces of sucrose and fructose obtained from the boiling and evaporation of sugarcane juice; a food staple in Colombia and other countries in South and Central America.
- *Molasses:* used as a sweetener and a syrup accompanying other foods, such as cheese or cookies.
- *Rapadura*: a sweet flour which is one of the simplest refinings of sugarcane juice.
- *Rum:* a liquor made of the distillation of sugarcane commonly produced in the Caribbean. Rum is more purified than the Brasilian *cachaça.*
- *Falernum:* a sweet, and lightly alcoholic drink made from sugar cane juice.
- *Syrup:* a traditional sweetener in soft drinks, now largely supplanted in the US by high fructose corn syrup, which is less expensive because of corn subsidies and sugar tariffs.
- *Sayur nganten*: an Indonesian soup made of trubuk stem (*Saccharum edule*).

CHAPTER - 11

Phragmites

Phragmites, the Common reed, is a large perennial grass found in wetlands throughout temperate and tropical regions of the world. *Phragmites australis* is sometimes regarded as the sole species of the genus *Phragmites*, though some botanists divide *Phragmites australis* into three or four species. In particular the South Asian Khagra Reed — *Phragmites karka* — is often treated as a distinct species.

The generally accepted botanical name of Common reed is *Phragmites australis* (Cav.) Trin. ex Steud.. However, it is still often known as *Phragmites communis* Trin.; other synonyms include *Arundo phragmites* L. (the basionym), *Phragmites altissimus, P. berlandieri, P. dioicus, P. maximus, P. vulgaris.*

Subspecies

Recent studies have characterised morphological distinctions between the introduced and native stands of *Phragmites* in North America. The Eurasian genotype can be distinguished from the North American genotype by its shorter ligules of up to 0.9 millimetres (0.04 in) as opposed to over 1.0 millimetre (0.04 in), shorter glumes of under 3.2 millimetres (0.13 in) against over 3.2 millimetres (0.13 in) (although there is some overlap in this character), and in culm characteristics.

- *Phragmites australis* subsp. *americanus*—Recently, the North American genotype has been described as a distinct subspecies, subsp. *americanus*; and
- *Phragmites australis* subsp. *australis* — the Eurasian variety is referred to as subsp. *australis*.

Native and Introduced Species

In North America, the status of *Phragmites australis* was a source of confusion and debate. It was commonly considered an exotic species and often invasive species, introduced from Europe. However now with evidence of the existence of *Phragmites* as a native plant in North America long before European colonization of the continent. It is now known that the North American native forms of *P. a.* subsp. *americanus* are markedly less vigorous than European forms. The recent marked expansion of *Phragmites* in North America may be due to the more vigorous, but otherwise almost indistinguishable European subsp. *australis*, best detectable by genetic analysis.

Phragmites australis subsp. *australis* is causing serious problems for many other North American hydrophyte wetland plants, including the native *Phragmites australis* subsp. *americanus*. Gallic acid released by Phragmites is degraded by ultraviolet light to produce mesoxalic acid, effectively hitting susceptible plants and seedlings with two harmful toxins. Phragmites are so difficult to control that one of the most effective methods of eradicating the plant is to burn it over 2-3 seasons. The roots grow so deep and strong that one burn is not enough.

Growth and Habitat

Phragmites australis, Common reed, commonly forms extensive stands (known as reed beds), which may be as much as 1 square kilometre (0.39 sq mi) or more in extent. Where conditions are suitable it can spread at 5 metres (16 ft) or more per year by horizontal runners, which put down roots at regular intervals. It can grow in damp ground, in standing water up to 1 metre (3 ft 3 in) or so deep, or even as a floating mat. The erect stems grow to 2-6 metres (6 ft 7 in-19 ft 8 in) tall, with the tallest plants growing in areas with hot summers and fertile growing conditions.

The leaves are long for a grass, 20-50 centimetres (7.9-20 in) and 2-3 centimetres (0.79-1.2 in) broad. The flowers are produced in late summer in a dense, dark purple panicle, about 20-50 cm long. Later the numerous long, narrow, sharp pointed spikelets appear greyer due to the growth of long, silky hairs.

It is a halophyte, especially common in alkaline habitats, and it also tolerates brackish water, and so is often found at the upper edges of estuaries and on other wetlands (such as grazing marsh) which are occasionally inundated by the sea.

Common reed is suppressed where it is grazed regularly by livestock. Under these conditions it either grows as small shoots within the grassland sward, or it disappears altogether.

In Europe, common reed is rarely invasive, except in damp grasslands where traditional grazing has been abandoned.

Common reed is very important (together with other reed-like plants) for wildlife and conservation, particularly in Europe and Asia, where several species of birds are strongly tied to large *Phragmites* stands. These include:

- Bearded Reedling (*Panurus biarmicus*)
- Reed Warbler (*Acrocephalus scirpaceus*)
- Great Bittern (*Botaurus stellaris*)

Phytoremediation Water Treatment

Phragmites australis is one of the main wetland plant species used for phytoremediation water treatment.

Waste water from lavatories and greywater from kitchens is routed to an underground septic tank-like compartment where the solid waste is allowed to settle out.

The water then trickles through a constructed wetland or *artificial reed bed*, where bioremediation bacterial action on the surface of roots and leaf litter removes some of the nutrients in biotransformation. The water is then suitable for irrigation, groundwater recharge, or release to natural watercourses.

Thatching

Reed is used in many areas for thatching roofs. In the British Isles, common reed used for this purpose is known as *Norfolk reed* or *water reed*. However 'wheat reed' and 'Devon reed', also used for thatching, are not in fact reed, but long-stemmed wheat straw.

Other Uses

Some other uses for *Phragmites australis* and other reeds in various cultures include baskets, mats, pen tips, and a rough form of paper.

In the Philippines, *Phragmites* is known by the local name 'tambo'. Reed stands flower in December, and the blooms are harvested and bundled into brooms called 'walis'. Hence the common name of household brooms is 'walis tambo'.

In Australian Aboriginal cultures, reeds were used to make weapons like spears for hunting game.

Food

Numerous parts of Phragmites can be prepared for consumption. For example, the young stems "while still green and fleshy, can be dried and pounded into a fine powder, which when moistened is roasted [sic] like marshmallows." Also, the wheat-like seeds on the apex of the stems "can be ground into flour or made into gruel." Rootstocks are used similarly.

Legend and Literature

When Midas had his ears transformed into donkey's ears, he concealed the fact and his barber was sworn to secrecy. However the barber could not contain himself and rather than confiding in another human, he spoke the secret into a hole in the ground. The reeds that grew in that place then repeated the secret in whispers.

Moses was "drawn out of the water where his mother had placed him in a reed basket to save him from the death that had been decreed by the Pharaoh against the firstborn of all of the children of Israel in Egypt" (Exodus 2:10). However, the plant concerned may have been another reed-like plant, such as papyrus, which is still used for making boats.

One reference to reeds in European literature is Frenchman Blaise Pascal's saying that Man is but a 'thinking reed'—*roseau pensant*. In Jean de La Fontaine's famous fable *The Oak and the Reed—Le chêne et le roseau*, the reed tells the proud oak: "I bend, and break not"—"*Je plie, et ne romps pas,*" 'before the tree's fall'.

Thatching

Thatching is the craft of building a roof with dry vegetation such as straw, water reed, sedge (Cladium mariscus), rushes and heather, layering the vegetation so as to shed water away from the inner roof. It is a very old roofing method and has been used in both tropical and temperate climates. Thatch is still employed by builders in developing countries, usually with low-cost, local vegetation. By contrast in some developed countries it is now the choice of affluent people who desire a rustic look for their home or who have purchased an originally thatched abode.

The tradition of thatching has been passed down from generation to generation for thousands of years, and numerous descriptions of the materials and methods used in England over the past three centuries survive in archives and early publications.

In equatorial countries thatch is the prevalent local material for roofs, and often walls. There are diverse building techniques from the ancient Hawaiian *hale* shelter made from the local ti leaves, lauhala or pili grass of fan palms to the Na Bure Fijian home with layered reed walls and sugar cane leaf roofs and the Kikuyu tribal homes in Kenya. The colonisation of indigenous lands by Europeans greatly diminished the use of thatching.

Thatch has probably been used to cover roofs in Europe since at least the Neolithic period, when people first began to grow cereals. Wild vegetation, especially water reed (Phragmites australis), was probably used before this but no records or archaeological evidence for this have survived".

Early settlers to the New World used thatch as far back as 1565. Native Americans had already been using thatch for generations. When settlers arrived in Jamestown, Virginia in 1607, they found Powhatan Indians living in houses with thatched roofs. The colonists used the same thatch on their own buildings.

In most of Europe and the UK, thatch remained the only roofing material available to the bulk of the population in the countryside, and in many towns and villages, until the late 1800s. The commercial production of Welsh slate had begun in 1820 and the mobility which the canals and then the railways made possible meant that other materials became readily available. The number of thatched properties actually increased in the UK during the mid-1800s as agriculture expanded, but then declined again at the end of the 19th century because of agricultural recession and rural depopulation. Gradually, thatch became a mark of poverty and the number of thatched properties gradually declined, as did the number of professional thatchers.

Thatch has become much more popular in the UK over the past 30 years, and is now a symbol of wealth rather than poverty. There are now approximately 1,000 full time thatchers at work in the UK, and thatching is becoming popular again because of the renewed interest in preserving historic buildings and using more sustainable building materials. There are more thatched roofs in the United Kingdom and Ireland than in any other European country. Good quality thatching straw can last for more than 45–50 years when applied by a skilled thatcher. Traditionally, a new layer of straw was simply applied over the weathered surface, and this 'spar coating' tradition has created accumulations of thatch over 7' (2.1m) thick on very old buildings. Over 250 roofs in Southern England have base coats of thatch that were applied over 500 years ago, providing direct evidence of the types of materials that were used for thatching in the medieval period. Almost all of these roofs are thatched with wheat, rye, or a 'maslin' mixture of both. Medieval wheat grew to almost 6 feet (1.8 m) tall in very poor soils and produced durable straw for the roof and grain for baking bread. Information on UK thatching materials, methods and traditions, and the work that is being done to preserve them, is available on the Conservation of Historic Thatch website.

Technology in the farming industry has had a significant impact on the popularity of thatching. The availability of good quality thatching straw declined in England after the introduction of the combine harvester in the late 1930s and 1940s, and the release of short-stemmed wheat varieties. The increasing use of nitrogen fertiliser in the 1960s-70s also weakened straw and reduced its longevity. Since the 1980s, however, there has been a big increase in straw quality as specialist growers have returned to growing older, tall-stemmed, 'heritage' varieties of wheat such as Maris Wigeon, in low input/organic conditions.

All of the evidence indicates that water reed was rarely used for thatching outside of East Anglia. It has traditionally been a 'one coat' material applied in a similar way to how it is used in continental Europe — weathered reed is usually stripped and replaced by a new layer. It takes 4-5 acres of well-managed reed bed to produce enough reed to thatch an average house, and large reed beds have been uncommon in most of England since the Anglo-Saxon period. Over 80 per cent of the water reed used in the UK is now imported from Turkey, Eastern Europe and China. Although water reed might last for 50 years or more on a steep roof in a dry climate, modern imported water reed on an average roof in

England will not last any longer than good quality wheat straw. The lifespan of a thatched roof is also dependent on the skill of the thatcher, but other factors need to be taken into account, such as climate, quality of the materials used, and the pitch of the roof.

Thatch is fastened together in bundles with a diameter of about two feet. These are then laid on the roof with the butt end facing out and secured to the roof beams, after which they are pegged in place with wooden or steel rods. The thatcher adds the layers on top of each other, finishing with a layer to secure the ridgeline of the roof. This method means thatch roofs are easy to repair, can endure heavy winds and rain and only need a stable supporting structure.

In areas where palms are abundant, palm leaves are used to thatch walls and roofs. Many species of palm trees are called 'thatch palm', or have 'thatch' as part of their common names. In the southeastern United States, Indian and pioneer houses were often constructed of palmetto-leaf thatch. The chickees of the Seminole and Miccosukee Indians are still thatched with palmetto leaves.

Good thatch will not require frequent maintenance. In England a ridge will normally last 10-15 years, and re-ridging will be required several times during the lifespan of a thatch. Covering thatch with wire netting is no longer recommended, as this will slow evaporation and reduce its longevity. Moss can be a problem if it is very thick, but is not usually detrimental.

The thickness of the thatch decreases over the years as the surface is gradually eroded. A thatched roof can be thought to be nearing replacement when the horizontal fixings of each course are close to the surface. "A roof is as good as the amount of correctly laid thatch covering the fixings".

Flammability

Thatch roofs do not catch fire any more frequently than roofs covered with 'hard' materials, but thatch fires are difficult to extinguish once they take hold. Old buildings often have poor quality chimneys, and most fires occur in the winter when hot gases ignite the thatch surrounding the chimney. Insurance premiums are higher than average because when a fire does occur, the damage is more severe and the thatch is more expensive to replace than a standard tiled/slate roof. Workmen should never be allowed to use an open flame near thatch, and nothing should be burnt that could fly up the chimney and ignite the surface of the thatch. Spark arrestors usually cause more damage than good as they are easily blocked and reduce air flow.

A spray-on fire retardant or pressure impregnated fire retardant is available that can reduce the spread of flame, and lower the radiated heat output of the fire.

On new buildings a solid fire retardant barrier can be applied over the rafters making the thatch sacrificial in case of fire. If fireboards are used, it is essential that a ventilation gap be left between the boarding and the thatch so that the roof can 'breathe', as condensation can be a significant problem in thin, single layer thatch. Condensation is much less of a problem on thick straw roofs, and because they do not need to be ventilated provide much better insulation. In Ireland and the Isle of Man, turf is laid upon the rafters to form a fire barrier and this is called 'scraw'.

Performance

The performance of thatch depends on roof shape and design, pitch of roof, position—its geography and topography—the quality of material and the expertise of the thatcher.

Thatch has some natural properties that are advantageous to its performance. It is naturally weather-resistant,and when properly maintained does not absorb a lot of water. There should not be a significant increase to roof weight due to water retention. A roof pitch of at least 50 degrees allows precipitation to travel quickly down slope so that it runs off the roof before it can penetrate the structure.

Thatch is also a natural insulator, and air pockets within straw thatch insulate a building in both warm and cold weather. A thatched roof will ensure that a building will be cool in summer and warm in winter.

Thatch also has very good resistance to wind damage when applied correctly.

Advantages

Thatching materials range from plains grasses to waterproof leaves found in equatorial regions. It is the most common roofing material in the world, because the materials are readily available.

Thatch is a versatile material when it comes to covering irregular roof structures. This fact lends itself to the use of second-hand, recycled and natural materials that are not only more sustainable, but need not fit exact standard dimensions to perform well.

Disadvantages

Thatched houses are harder to insure because of the perceived fire risk, and because thatching is labour intensive it is much more expensive to thatch a roof than to cover it with slate or tiles. Birds can damage a roof while they are foraging for grubs, and rodents are attracted by residual grain in straw.

Thatch has fallen out of favour in much of the industrialised world not because of fire, but because thatching has become very expensive and alternative 'hard' materials are cheaper—but this situation is slowly changing. There are almost 100,000 thatched roofs in the UK, and many more are being built every year.

New thatched roofs were forbidden in London by the Normans in the 12th century, and existing roofs had to have their surfaces plastered to reduce the risk of fire. The Great Fire of London in 1666 had nothing to do with thatch. The modern Globe Theatre is one of the few thatched buildings in London (others can be found in the suburb of Kingsbury), but the Globe's modern, water reed thatch is purely for decorative purpose and actually lies over a fully waterproofed roof built with modern materials. The Globe Theatre, opened in 1997, was modeled on the Rose which was destroyed by a fire on a dry June night in 1613 when a burning wad of cloth ejected from a special effects canon during a performance set light to the surface of the thatch.

Reed Bed

Reed beds are natural habitats found in floodplains, waterlogged depressions and estuaries. Reed beds are part of a succession from young reed colonising open water or wet ground through a gradation of increasingly dry ground. As reed beds age, they build up a considerable litter layer which eventually rises above the water level, and ultimately provides opportunities for scrub or woodland invasion. Artificial reed beds are used as a method of removing pollutants from grey water.

Reed beds vary in the species they can support, depending on water levels within the wetland system, climate, seasonal variations, and the nutrient status and salinity of the water. Those that normally have 20 cm or more of surface water during the summer are referred to as *reed swamp*. These often have high invertebrate and bird species use. Reed beds with water levels at or below the surface during the summer are often more complex botanically and are known as *reed fen*. Reeds and similar plants do not generally grow in very acidic water, and so in these situations reed beds are replaced by other vegetation such as poor-fen and bog.

Although common reed is characteristic of reed beds, not all vegetation dominated by this species is reed bed. It also occurs commonly in unmanaged damp grassland and as an understorey in certain types of damp woodland.

Wildlife

Most European reed beds are composed mainly of the large wetland grass common reed (*Phragmites australis*), but also include many other tall monocotyledons adapted to growing in wet conditions – other grasses such as reed sweet-grass (*Glyceria maxima*), Canary reed-grass (*Phalaris arundinacea*) and small-reed (*Calamagrostis* species), large sedges (species of *Carex, Scirpus, Schoenoplectus, Cladium* and related genera), yellow flag iris (*Iris pseudacorus*), reed-mace ("bulrush" – *Typha* species), water-plantains (*Alisma* species), and flowering rush (*Butomus umbellatus*). Many dicotyledons also occur, such as water mint (*Mentha aquatica*), gipsywort (*Lycopus europaeus*), skull-cap (*Scutellaria* species), touch-me-not balsam (*Impatiens noli-tangere*), brooklime (*Veronica beccabunga*) and water forget-me-nots (*Myosotis* species). Many animals are adapted to living in and around reed-beds. These include mammals such as Eurasian otter, European beaver, water vole, harvest mouse and water shrew, and birds such as Great Bittern, Purple Heron, European Spoonbill, Water Rail (and other rails), Purple Gallinule, Marsh Harrier, various warblers (Reed Warbler, Sedge Warbler etc), Bearded Reedling and Reed Bunting.

Constructed wetlands are artificial swamps (sometimes called *reed fields*) using reed or other marshland plants to form part of small-scale sewage treatment systems. Water trickling through the reed bed is cleaned by microorganisms living on the root system and in the litter. These utilising the sewage for growth nutrients, resulting in a clean effluent. The process is very similar to aerobic conventional sewage treatment, as the same organisms are used, except that conventional treatment systems require artificial aeration.

Treatment Ponds

Treatment ponds are small versions of constructed wetlands which uses reed beds or other marshland plants to form an even smaller water treatment system. Similar to constructed wetlands, water trickling through the reed bed is cleaned by microorganisms living on the root system and in the litter. Treatment ponds are used for the water treatment of a single house or a small neighbourhood.

CHAPTER – 12

Laying Sod

To start new lawns, many people wonder which is better: laying sod or sowing grass seed. While seeding is cheaper and offers a wider variety of grass types, many people are won over to laying sod by two convincing arguments: laying sod is fast and produces high-quality new lawns. In fact, laying sod is so fast, it's fair to say it gives you an 'instant lawn'. Check with your county extension to learn which grass types are best for your region.

Remove the old lawn and/or weeds, if any exist. One way to accomplish this is by digging them out with a flat-bladed shovel (make sure you get the roots). Another method is to apply an herbicide, then rent a sod-cutter to remove roots and all. Before proceeding further, have your soil pH tested. Most lawn grasses prefer a pH of 6.0 to 7.5. If the test reveals that you need to adjust the pH, do so in conjunction with Step # 2. Break up the compacted soil with a tiller. Tillers (also called rototillers) can be rented from your local rental center. Spread a starter fertilizer over the now-loosened soil. This type of fertilizer is high in phosphorus, the middle number in the NPK sequence on a fertilizer bag.

Also spread a soil conditioner over the soil. 'Soil conditioner' is often what it's called at the store, but if you have a good supply of compost at home, it will serve just as well as a soil amendment. Again using the tiller, till the starter fertilizer and soil conditioner (or equivalent) into the soil. I know this seems like a lot of work, but good soil preparation is one key to success in laying sod to start new lawns. Now rake the soil to begin to level it out, removing any rocks and debris that you find. To avoid problems with excess water-runoff, make sure that any site grading you do allows water to flow away from your house. This step requires a roller. Rollers, like tillers, can be rented from your local rental centre. Fill the roller's drum with water, then use the roller to finish leveling the soil. Start laying your sod. Begin on the outer edges, unrolling a roll of sod on the far left-hand side, then another on the far right-hand side (or vice versa). After laying these 2 rolls of sod, work your way in towards the centre with subsequent strips. A single roll of sod may not be long enough to cover the whole length of the lawn. This means you'll have to lay separate rolls, end to end, pressing the ends firmly together so that they abut tightly, but without overlapping.

For the strips of sod in the adjacent row, make sure you stagger the ends of sod rolls, so that the seams don't line up. Think of it as a 'brickwork' pattern.

If a strip of sod appears too low, 'shim' it with topsoil to bring it up to the proper level.

When you're done laying sod, it's time to use the roller again. Push it over the sod to press it down firmly against the soil. This removes air pockets, promoting good contact with the soil, allowing your sod's roots to go to work immediately.

For a couple of weeks after laying sod, remember to water faithfully every day. If you know your schedule won't permit this, now's the time to look into automatic irrigation systems, before starting a new lawn.

Tips

In Step # 8, I had you begin laying sod on the edges first. Why? Because the sod on the edges has the greatest tendency to dry out. By starting on the edges, you ensure that the edges will at least have sod strips of the full width, making them less likely to dry out. When you get to the center, sod widths may have to be trimmed (use a sharp knife). But better there than on the edges, for the reason just stated. In a nutshell: you may have to trim somewhere, so make sure it's not on the edges.

What's the best time for laying sod? Your supplier will have the most accurate info on this topic, since they're experts on the grass type you'll be purchasing. They will also know when it's best to lay sod in your area. Obviously, Step # 2 can only be executed during those times of the year when the ground is not frozen. At the other extreme, mid-summer is less than ideal for starting new lawns, since the extreme heat makes drying out more likely. Early fall and early spring are the best times.

If, instead of laying sod, you prefer the seeding method, see my tips for seeding lawns. The first 7 steps (soil preparation) are the same as for starting new lawns via the sodding method.

What You Need:

- Tiller (Rototiller)
- Roller
- Sod
- Starter Fertilizer
- Soil Conditioner
- Rake
- Sharp Knife
- (Depending on option selected in Step # 1) Either a flat-bladed shovel
- Herbicide and a sod-cutter.

Sod or *turf* is grass and the part of the soil beneath it held together by the roots, or a piece of thin material.

The term *sod* may be used to mean turf grown and cut specifically for the establishment of lawns. However, in British English such material is more usually known as *turf*, and the word 'sod' is limited mainly to agricultural senses (for example for turf when ploughed), or avoided altogether, due to the alternative offensive meaning of the word 'sod'.

Sod (or turf) for lawns is grown on specialist farms. It is usually grown locally to avoid long transport and drying out and heat buildup of the product. It is sold to landscapers, home builders or home owners who use it to establish a lawn quickly and avoid soil erosion. The farms that produce this grass may have many varieties of grass grown in one location to best suit the consumer's use and preference of appearance. It is usually harvested 10 to 18 months after planting, depending on the growing climate. On the farm it undergoes fertilization, frequent watering, frequent mowing and subsequent vacuuming to remove the clippings. It is harvested using specialized equipment, precision cut to standardized sizes. Sod is typically harvested in small square slabs, rolled rectangles, or large 4-foot-wide (1.2 m) rolls. Some large sod farms may export internationally. Because of the product's short life after harvest, the sod may be washed clean of the soil down to the bare roots (or sprigs) which makes shipping lighter and cheaper. Sod can be used to repair a small area of lawn that has died.

Sodding *Versus* Seeding

Seed may be blown about by the wind, eaten by birds, or fail because of drought. It takes some weeks to form a visually appealing lawn, and further time before it is robust enough for use.

Turf largely avoids these problems, and with proper care, newly laid sod is usually fully functional within 30 days of installation and its root system is comparable to that of a seeding lawn two or three years older.

Turf is however more expensive, and requires considerably more water for its establishment. Erosion after seeding may be a concern in some areas near water. Sod reduces erosion by stabilizing the soil in these type of areas.

Cost

Different types of sod will have different pricing. The availability of sod grasses is generally dependent on where the lawn is located climate-wise. For the United States, landscapers in the northern states will generally sod a lawn with either Kentucky bluegrass or tall fescue. Kentucky bluegrass has a nice deep green color to it, while tall fescue though not as deep green is excellent for areas that receive medium to heavy traffic since it can resist a lot of abuse. The best, some claim, is a compromise between the two, namely, a grass mixture. Mixtures are also preferred because of disease. "Most [grass] diseases will only strike one type of grass, so the damage will probably be limited [when the lawn was built based on a grass mixture]." Mixed grass sod is sold containing a percentage of Kentucky bluegrass, tall fescue, and/or ryegrass to fill this need.

Laying Sod Grass

By laying sod one can have an instantly grassy and lush yard. You can install sod yourself, although it does require planning and work.

Order the sod, so that you can lay it as soon as the ground is prepared. But do not have it delivered or pick it up before preparations are complete; sod rots if it sits in the sun for too long before you lay it. For best results, plan on laying sod the same day it arrives.

First, prepare the soil:

Get rid of existing weeds and grasses on the site. Use a herbicide that does not leave a toxic residue.

Till the lawn area, and clear it of rocks and other debris.

Test the pH of the soil. You can have your soil's pH tested by a garden centre or agricultural extension or you can buy an inexpensive *soil pH test kit.*

If needed, as determined by soil testing, apply organic amendments and/or top soils to change the soil composition and texture.

Wait a week, then spread any initial soil fertilizers and till your lawn area a second time. At this time, also install any lawn sprinkler systems, sidewalks, or other walk/patio surfaces that you want in your lawn.

Do a final rake or drag of the area before laying sod to ensure that the ground is level and that all larger pebbles, rocks, and sticks are removed from the area.

Now that the soil is ready, proceed to laying sod.

Water the lawn area the day before your sod arrives. Use several short irrigations, an hour apart, to soak the ground to a depth of 15 cm (6 inches) or more while preventing runoff. This will allow the sod to root more quickly.

Install sod along the longest straight line from back to front. (A sidewalk, driveway, or flowerbed against the side of the house makes an excellent guide.) Follow these guidelines:

- Work from this straight line to avoid stepping on the freshly placed sod.
- Butt edges and ends together tightly.
- Lay strips of sod in a brick pattern (staggering the locations of joints) to minimize visible lines while the sod takes root.
- Avoid splicing curved and angled areas with small pieces and strips. The bigger the piece, the better it will root.
- Use a sharp sod knife to make clean, defined edges around trees, sprinklers, and contours.

After laying sod, go over it with lawn roller. The roller, which you can rent, is specially designed to help sodded lawns take better root by forcing the roots in the sod to make contact with the soil below.

Water thoroughly after laying sod. Keep new sod very wet for 10 days to 2 weeks. Water 3 to 6 times a day depending on the weather. After a week or so, check rooting progress by gently tugging on individual strips. If the sod doesn't come up easily, the rooting process is well under way. If the sod hasn't begun to root or shows gray, dry looking areas, increase the water. Keep foot traffic off the sod until it is well-rooted.

After laying sod, take care of it:

Keep grass height high for the first few cuttings. Let it reach a height of 10 to 12 cm (4 to 4.75 inches) before mowing. Take two cm (0.75 inch) off the top, wait a few days, and do it again. Mow when grass blades are dry, then water the grass. Low-cutting new sod can disturb the strips and damage new roots.

After the sod is established, usually a month or so, water according to weather and soil conditions. Watch the weather and adjust to establish a responsible, efficient watering schedule. Watch your lawn carefully, check water coverage, adjust sprinklers as needed, and use hand watering to deal with any 'hot spots' (smoky gray areas) that arise during hot or windy weather.

Fertilize lightly after the second mowing with a seasonal lawn fertilizer. To avoid changing fertilizers every season, use a premium lawn food that conditions your soil while providing long-lasting, complete, and balanced nutrition for your grass year-round.

Prairie Grasses

San Rafael Gran Sabana, Venezuela Savanna of Venezuela

Rolled Sod

Indoor Grown Wheatgrass Grows from 8-14 Days Before it is Harvested

Uncut Grass

Grass Used as an Ornamental Planting

Meadow Fescue (*Festuca Pratensis*)

Straw-thatched House in Japan

Lolium temulentum (Poison Darnel)

Sugarcane Plantation in Pakistan

Grassland in Cantabria, Northern Spain

View of the Northern Pampas Grain Belt

European Marram Grass

Bamboo Plants Growing in the Philippines

Napier Grass Planted Using Conventional Methods

Livestock Feeding on Dry Natural Grass
during Severe Drought

Lemon Grass Plant

Tall Napier Grass

Bamboo Foliage with Yellow Stems

Sugarcane Field on Madeira

Tundra Region with Fjords, Glaciers and Mountains. Kongsfjorden, Spitsbergen

Grass Covered House in Iceland

Grass Grown to Prevent Erosion

Bunch-tussock Grasses in the Konza Tallgrass Prairie

Extracting Wheatgrass Juice with a Manual Juicing Machine

A Garden with a Lawn

Agrostis capillaris

Creeping Bentgrass

CHAPTER – 13

Long Grass Plantation

Long Grass Plantation is located along what was the Roanoke River basin but in the 1950s became the Buggs Island Lake/ John H. Kerr Reservoir in Mecklenburg County, Virginia. Built circa 1800 by George Tarry on land belonging to his father, Samuel Tarry (said land being named Ivy Hill, house razed in the 1950s), Long Grass Plantation encompassed approximately 2000 acres (8 km^2). Today, most of the land once belonging to Long Grass is submerged and is owned by the US Army Corps of Engineers. Only 27 +/- acres of privately owned land make up the grounds of Long Grass. The property was listed on the Virginia Landmarks Registry and the National Register of Historic Places on July 21, 1995.

The original hall and parlour structure still exists and has been added on to over the years in 4 major phases.

The current structure is dominated by the additions made in the early to mid 19th century by builder-architect Jacob W. Holt of Warrenton, NC. In the early 1830s Holt was commissioned to build a 2-storey, single-pile, 3-bay addition to the front of the original 1.5 storey house. The 2 structures were connected via a 1-storey hyphen. The addition is much larger in scale and massing than the original hall and parlour and with a neoclassical entrance and porch (probably salvaged from and earlier home in Warren County or along the Roanoke River) the newer addition was an indication of the economic fortune generated from tobacco cultivation. Several years later (probably in the late 1840s) Holt was again commissioned to make improvements to the property. By this time Holt had adopted elements of the popular Italianate style of architecture in his designs. Holt raised the roof of the original hall and parlor to make a full second storey and designed a relatively ornate single storey porch across the rear of the house.

A rear view of the main structure showing the original hall and parlor house enlarged with a second storey and an ornate rear porch.

In the 1950s the house was renovated and retrofitted with modern mechanical systems. The 1-storey hyphen connecting the two structures was raised to 2 full stories. Two new bathrooms were created — one upstairs in the new hyphen space and one downstairs in the Holt addition dining room space.

The most recent renovation occurred in the 1990s when Bruce and Sudie Park of Raleigh, North Carolina purchased the property. Michael Denton of Clarksville, Virginia and Trent Park managed the renovation project. At this time the property was completely renovated and the spaces between the original hall and parlour and the Holt addition on either side of the hyphen were enclosed to make space for a breakfast room, study, and 2 new bathrooms upstairs. The bathroom created in the 1950s in the Holt dining room was removed completely. New, updated mechanical systems were installed.

On the grounds of Long Grass Plantation are many of the buildings historically used by the plantation to carry out domestic and agricultural tasks. Of the original historic structures the Ice House, Smoke House, Kitchen/Laundry, School House, Pack House, 2 Tobacco Barns, and a Double Tennant (former slave) Dwelling still exist. Of these buildings the Tennant House is in the most advanced state of decay. The Pack House is also nearing disrepair. All of the other buildings are structurally sound and well protected.

Items of note:

- The frame Ice House (ca. 1830) is most unusual. It is very large for an Ice House or Dairy Building. The structure is 2 stories with a pit underneath. Over time it has been used to store corn and the second storey was used as a pigeon coop.
- The one-room School House (ca. 1800) was renovated and added on to in the 1950s to create a cottage with kitchen, bathroom and sleeping loft.
- The Smoke House (ca. 1830) was noted in 19th century letters as being one of the largest and most secure in the region. It most recently was used to house poultry
- The Kitchen/Laundry (ca. 1830 and 1840) actually began as a kitchen only. Built of frame construction it had a brick floor and a massive stone firebox and chimney. Later (probably when Holt added the rear porch) the structure was doubled in size by adding on behind the chimney. A fireplace was created in the addition that shared the original chimney. Today the laundry room fireplace and the original chimney still stand but the original enormous stone fireplace in the kitchen building has collapsed.

The Tobacco Pack House has suffered some serious structural damage but still stands and is relatively well protected. This is the building where the tobacco was stored and processed for drying and transportation to market. The structure was added on to over time. In its current configuration it is roughly rectangular with 4 irregularly shaped rooms on the first storey and a large loft area above. There are very few window openings. There is a large stone lined humidor pit underneath a portion of the structure that was used for managing the moisture level of the leaves. The land on which Long Grass Plantation was built by Tarry was granted by King George to his father for the building of Ivy Hill. A third plantation named Wildwood was built upon this land by a Tarry son.

Planted in the front yard of Long Grass is a 'Constitution Oak' from the 1912 Virginia Constitutional Convention. The Burr Oak is an unusual species in Virginia. Each of the delegates to this constitutional convention were given a sapling to plant to commemorate the event.

Wheatgrass

Wheatgrass is a food prepared from the cotyledons of the common wheat plant, *Triticum aestivum*. It is sold either as a juice or powder concentrate. Wheatgrass differs from wheat malt in that it is served freeze-dried or fresh, while wheat malt is convectively dried. Wheatgrass is also allowed to grow longer than malt is. It provides chlorophyll, amino acids, minerals, vitamins, and enzymes. Claims about the health benefits of wheatgrass range from providing supplemental nutrition to having unique curative properties. Some consumers grow and juice wheatgrass in their homes. It is often available in juice bars, alone or in mixed fruit or vegetable drinks. It is also available in many health food stores as fresh produce, tablets, frozen juice and powder.

The consumption of wheatgrass in the Western world began in the 1930s as a result of experiments conducted by Charles F. Schnabel in his attempts to popularize the plant.

Schnabel, an agricultural chemist, conducted his first experiments with young grasses in 1930, when he used fresh cut grass in an attempt to nurse dying hens back to health. The hens not only recovered, but they produced eggs at a higher rate than healthy hens. Encouraged by his results, he began drying and powdering grass for his family and neighbors to supplement their diets. The following year, Schnabel reproduced his experiment and achieved the same results. Hens consuming rations supplemented with grass doubled their egg production. Schnabel started promoting his discovery to gristmills, chemists and the food industry.

Two large corporations, Quaker Oats and American Dairies Inc., invested millions of dollars in further research, development, and production of grass products for animals and humans. By 1940, cans of Schnabel's powdered grass were on sale in major drug stores throughout the United States and Canada.

Schnabel's research was conducted with wheatgrass grown outdoors in Kansas. His wheatgrass required 200 days of slow growth, through the winter and early spring, when it was harvested at the jointing stage. It is at this stage that the plant reached its peak nutritional value; after jointing, concentrations of chlorophyll, protein, and vitamins decline sharply. Harvested grass was dehydrated and made into powders and tablets for human and animal consumption. Wheatgrass grown indoors in trays for ten days contains similar nutritional content. Wheatgrass grown outdoors is harvested, dehydrated at a low temperature and sold in tablet and powdered concentrates. Wheat grass juice powder (freshly squeezed with the water removed) is also available either spray-dried or freeze-dried.

Indoor Growing and Mold

Growing wheat grass indoors usually requires the grass to be grown in small trays with the wheat grains close together for a high yield. Not every wheat seed will sprout. Ungerminated seeds can develop mold which may spread to nearby sprouted plants. This may cause an unpalatable taste and, in extreme cases, an allergic reaction. This issue is not necessarily a problem when growing wheat in a field, due to less crowding of seeds and the resulting improved air circulation.

Usage

The average dosage taken by consumers of wheatgrass is 3.5 grams (powder or tablets). Some also have a fresh-squeezed 30 ml shot once daily or, for more therapeutic benefits, a higher dose up to 2-4 oz (60-120 ml) taken 1-3 times per day on an empty stomach and before meals. For detoxification, some users may increase their intake to 3-4 times per day. Consumers with a poor diet may experience nausea on high dosages of wheatgrass.

Proponents of wheatgrass make many claims for its health properties, ranging from promotion of general well-being to cancer prevention and heavy-metal detoxification. These claims have not been satisfactorily substantiated in the scientific literature, although there is some evidence in support of the beneficial effects of chlorophyll in the human diet. Some research exists that relates diets high in chlorophyll, present in higher concentrations in green leafy vegetables, to lower rates of colon cancer.

There are a number of other small studies and pilots on the possible benefits of wheatgrass juice. According to Memorial Sloan Kettering Cancer Centre, there may be a need for further study of wheatgrass therapy for ulcerative collitis; they cite a small pilot study which showed regular wheatgrass juice therapy significantly reduced rectal bleeding and overall disease activity.

It has been argued that wheatgrass helps blood flow, digestion and general detoxification of the body. These claims have not been reliably substantiated. However, in one pilot study of children with thalassaemia (a hereditary form of anemia which often requires blood transfusions), of the patients who were given 100ml of wheatgrass juice daily, half showed reduced need for transfusions. No adverse effects were observed. Another small study of transfusion-dependent patients suffering from myelodysplastic syndrome responded similarly to wheatgrass therapy; that is, the intervals between needed transfusions were increased. In addition, the chelation effect (removal of heavy metals from the blood) was studied for the same patients; the wheatgrass therapy showed a significant iron chelation effect.

In another pilot, breast cancer patients who drank wheatgrass juice daily showed a decreased need for blood-

and bone marrow-building medications during chemotherapy, without diminishing the effects of the therapy.

Wheatgrass proponent Schnabel claimed in the 1940s that "fifteen pounds of wheatgrass is equal in overall nutritional value to 350 pounds of ordinary garden vegetables", a ratio of 1:23. Despite claims of vitamin and mineral content disproportional to other vegetables, the nutrient content of wheatgrass juice is roughly equivalent to that of common vegetables.

Wheatgrass is also thought to be superior to other vegetables in its content of Vitamin B_{12}, a vital nutrient. Contrary to popular belief, B_{12} is not contained within wheat grass or any vegetable, rather it is a byproduct of the microorganisms living on plants. If plants are washed prior to consumption the water soluble B_{12} will be removed making most plants unreliable sources of B_{12}.

CHAPTER – 14

Organic Lawn Management

Organic lawn management is the practice of establishing and caring for a garden lawn using organic horticulture, without the use of chemical inputs such as pesticides or artificial fertilisers. It is a component of organic land care and organic sustainable landscaping which adapt the principles and methods of sustainable gardening and organic farming to the care of lawns and gardens.

Alternatives include the use of beneficial insects and natural predators such as nematodes to prevent infestation of lawns with pests such as crane fly larvae and ants, and preventing fungal infections through physical maintenance such as effective mowing and raking. Other 'environment friendly' techniques for caring for a lawn include irrigation only when the lawn shows signs of drought stress and then watering deeply-minimizing needless water consumption. Using low volume sprinklers provides more penetration without runoff. Lawnmowers with a mulching function can useful in reducing fertilizer use by allowing clippings that are cut so minutely that they can settle into the grass inconspicuously to decompose into the soil.

Organic Fertilizers

A primary element of organic lawn management is the use of compost and compost tea to reduce the need for fertilization and to encourage healthy soil that enables turf to resist pests. A second element is mowing tall (3"-4") to suppress weeds and encourage deep grass roots, and leaving grass clippings on the lawn as fertilizer. Additionally, fertilize in the fall, not the spring.

Synthetic (inorganic based) fertilizers are made in a chemical process that uses fossil fuel and contributes to global warming. They also greatly increase the amount of nitrogen entering the global nitrogen cycle which has a serious negative impact on the organization and functioning of the world's ecosystems, including accelerating the loss of biological diversity and decline of coastal marine ecosystems and fisheries. Nitrogen fertilizer releases N_2O, a greenhouse gas, into the atmosphere after application. Organic fertilizer nitrogen content is typically lower than synthetic fertilizer.

Biodiversity

Organic lawns contribute to biodiversity, by definition, when they contain more than one or two grass species. Examples of additional lawn and grasslike species that can be encouraged in organic lawns include dozens of grass species (eight for ryegrass alone, sedges, mosses, clover, vetches, trefoils, yarrow, ground cover alternatives, and other mowable plants. Biodiversity increases the functioning and stress tolerance of ecosystems. Lack of biodiversity is a significant environmental issue brought up by the use of lawns with grassroots groups emerging to promote this method of lawn care.

Lawn

A lawn is an area of aesthetic and recreational land planted with grasses or other durable plants, which usually are maintained at a low and consistent height. Low ornamental meadows in natural landscaping styles are a contemporary option of a lawn. In recreational contexts, the specialised names turf, pitch, field or green may be used, depending on the sport and the continent.

Lawns are a common feature of private gardens, public landscapes and parks in many parts of the world. They are created for aesthetic pleasure, as well as for sports or other outdoor recreational use. Lawns are useful as a playing surface both because they mitigate erosion and dust generated by intensive foot traffic and because they provide a cushion for players in sports such as rugby, football, soccer, cricket, baseball, golf, tennis, hockey and lawn bocce.

Lawns may have originated as grassed enclosures within early medieval settlements used for communal grazing of livestock, as distinct from fields reserved for agriculture. The word 'laune' is first attested in 1540, and is likely related to the Celtic Brythonic word *lan/llan/laun*, which has the meaning of enclosure, often in relation to a place of worship. Lawns became popular with the aristocracy in northern Europe from the Middle Ages onward. The early lawns were not always distinguishable from pasture fields. It is speculated the association between the word 'pasture' and biblical mentions made lawns a cultural affinity for some. The damp climate of maritime Western Europe in the north made lawns possible to grow and manage. They were not a part of gardens in other regions and cultures of the world until contemporary influence.

Before the invention of mowing machines in 1830, lawns were managed very differently. They were an element of wealthy estates and manor houses, and in some places were maintained by the labor-intensive methods of scything and shearing. In most situations, they were also pasture land maintained through grazing by sheep or other livestock. Areas of grass grazed regularly by rabbits, horses or sheep over a long period often form a very low, tight sward similar to a modern lawn. This was the original meaning of the word 'lawn', and the term can still be found in place names. Some forest areas where extensive grazing is practiced still have these seminatural lawns. For example, in the New Forest, England, such grazed areas are common, and are known as lawns, for example Balmer Lawn.

It was not until the Tudor and Elizabethan times that the garden and the lawn became a place created first as walkways and social areas. They were made up of meadow plants, such as camomile, a particular favorite. In the early 17th century, the Jacobean epoch of gardening began; during this period, the closely-cut 'English' lawn was born. By the end of this period, the English lawn was a symbol of status of the aristocracy and gentry.

In the early 18th century, landscape gardening entered another design style. William Kent and Lancelot 'Capability' Brown brought the landscape garden style into popularity. Lawns appeared to flow from the garden into the outer reaches of the estate landscape. The open 'English style' of parkland first spread across Britain and Ireland, and then across Europe, such as the *Garden à la française* being replaced by the French landscape garden.

After the U.S. Civil War, in the 1870s, lawns began to appear beyond affluent properties and city parks. Most people had neither the hired labour nor leisure time to cut a field of grass with scythes, and most raised vegetables and flowers. During the Victorian era, as more plants were introduced and available horticulturally in Europe, lawns became smaller, as flower beds were created and filled with perennials, sculptures, and water features. At the end of the 19th century, suburban development with land around residences began. With sprinkler technology, improved and mass-produced lawn mowers, new expectations about gardens, and a shorter working weeks, lawns came of age in the U.S. and northern Europe. Through the 20th century, western landscape influence brought the lawn to many parts of the world.

Lawns need not be, and have not always been, made up of grasses alone. Other plants for lawn-like usable garden areas are sedges, low herbs and wildflowers, and ground covers that can be walked upon.

Thousands of varieties of grasses and grasslike plants are used for lawns, each adapted to specific conditions of precipitation and irrigation, seasonal temperatures, and sun/shade tolerances. Plant hybridizers and botanists are constantly creating and finding improved varieties of the basic species and new ones, often more economical and environmentally sustainable by needing less water, fertilizer, pest and disease treatments, and maintenance. The three basic categories are cool season grasses, warm season grasses, and grass alternatives.

Grasses

Many different species of grass are used, depending on the intended use and the climate. Coarse grasses are used where active sports are played, and finer grasses are used for ornamental lawns for their visual effects. Some grasses are adapted to oceanic climates with cooler summers, and others to tropical and continental climates with hotter summers. Often, a mix of grass or low plant types is used to form a stronger lawn when one type does better in the warmer seasons and the other in the colder ones.

Cool Season Grasses

Cool season grasses start growth at 5°C (41°F), and grow at their fastest rate when temperatures are between 10°C (50°F) and 25°C (77°F), in climates that have relatively mild/cool summers, with two periods of rapid growth in the spring and autumn. They retain their colour well in extreme cold and typically grow very dense, carpetlike lawns with relatively little thatch.

Conventional selections:

- Bluegrass (*Poa* spp.)
- Bentgrass (*Agrostis* spp.)
- Ryegrasses (*Lolium* spp.)
- Fescues (*Festuca* spp., hybrids, and cultivars)

Native plant regional selections (for taller lawns):

- Red fescues (*Festuca rubra*)
- Feather reed grass (*Calamogrostis* spp.)
- Tufted hair grass (*Deschampsia* spp.)

Warm Season Grasses

Warm season grasses only start growth at temperatures above 10°C (50°F), and grow fastest when temperatures are between 25°C (77°F) and 35°C (95°F), with one long growth period over the spring and summer. They often go dormant in cooler months, turning shades of tan or brown. Many warm season grasses are quite drought tolerant, and can handle very high summer temperatures, although temperatures below -15°C (5.0°F) can kill most southern ecotype warm season grasses. The northern varieties, such as buffalograss and blue grama, are hardy to 45°C (113°F).

- Zoysiagrass (*Zoysia* spp.)
- Bermudagrass (*Cynodon* spp.)
- St. Augustine grass
- Bahiagrass (*Paspalum*)
- Centipedegrass (*Eremachloa*)
- Carpetgrass (*Axonopus*)
- Buffalograss (drought tolerant)
- Grama grass

Grass Alternatives

Carex species and cultivars are well represented in the horticulture industry as 'sedge' alternatives for 'grass' in mowed lawns and garden meadows. Both low growing and spreading ornamental cultivars and native species are used in for sustainable landscaping as low maintenance and drought tolerant grass replacements for lawns and garden meadows. wildland habitat restoration projects and natural landscaping and gardens use them also for 'user friendly' areas. The J. Paul Getty Museum has used *Carex pansa* (meadow sedge) and *Carex praegracilis* (dune sedge) expansively in the Sculpture Gardens in Los Angeles.

Some lower sedges used are:

- *Carex caryophyllea* (cultivar 'The Beatles')
- *C. divulsa* (Berkeley sedge)
- *C. glauca* (blue sedge) (syn. *C. flacca*)
- *C. pansa* (meadow sedge)
- *C. praegracilis* (dune sedge)
- *C. subfusca* (mountain sedge)
- *C. tumulicola* (foothill sedge) (cultivar 'Santa Cruz Mnts. selection')
- C. uncifolia (ruby sedge)

Ground Cover Alternatives

Some lawns are replaced with low ground covers, such as creeping thyme, camomile, *Lippia*, purple flowering *Mazus*, grey *Dymondia*, creeping sedums, and creeping jenny. Other alternatives to lawns include meadows, drought tolerant xeriscape gardens, natural landscapes, native plant habitat gardens, paved Spanish courtyard and patio gardens, butterfly gardens, rain gardens, and kitchen gardens. Trees and shrubs in close proximity to lawns provide habitat for birds in traditional, cottage and wildlife gardens.

Lawn Care and Maintenance

Seasonal lawn establishment and care varies depending on the climate zone and type of lawn grown.

Planting

Early autumn, spring, and early summer are the primary seasons to seed, lay sod, plant 'liners', or 'sprig' new lawns, when the soil is warmer and air cooler. Seeding is the least expensive, but takes longer for the lawn to establish; deeper rooting, though, can make for a more durable lawn. Sodding provides an almost 'instant lawn', and can be planted in most temperate climates in any season, but is more expensive and more vulnerable to drought. Hydroseeding is a quick, less expensive method of planting large, sloped or hillside landscapes. Some grasses and sedges are available and planted from 'liner' and 4 inch containers, from 'flats', 'plugs' or 'sprigs', and are planted apart to grow together.

Maintenance

Various organic and inorganic or synthetic fertilizers are available, with instant or time-release applications. Pesticides, which includes biological and chemical herbicides, insecticides and fungicides, are available. Consideration for their effects on the lawn and garden ecosystem, and via runoff and dispersion on the surrounding environment, can constrain their use. For example, the Canadian province of Quebec and over 130 municipalities prohibit the use of synthetic lawn pesticides. The Ontario provincial government promised on September 24, 2007 to also implement a province-wide ban on the cosmetic use of lawn pesticides, for protecting the public. Medical and environmental groups support such a ban. On April 22, 2008, the Provincial Government of Ontario announced that it will pass legislation that will prohibit, province-wide, the cosmetic use and sale of lawn and garden pesticides. The Ontario legislation would also echo Massachusetts law requiring pesticide manufacturers to reduce the toxins they use in production.

Sustainable gardening uses organic horticulture methods, such as organic fertilizers, biological pest control, beneficial insects, and companion planting, among other methods, to sustain an attractive lawn in a safe garden. An example of an organic herbicide is corn gluten meal, which releases an 'organic dipeptide' into the soil to inhibit root formation of germinating weed seeds. An insecticide alternative example is applying beneficial nematodes to combat grubs. The Integrated Pest Management approach is a coordinated low impact approach.

Mowing

Maintaining a rough lawn requires only occasional cutting with a suitable machine, or grazing by animals. Social pressure from neighbors and local municipal ordinances commonly require homeowners to keep grass cut.

Summer lawn care requires raising the lawn mower for cool season grasses, and lowering it for warm season lawns. Lawns will require longer and more frequent watering, best done in early morning to encourage a stronger root system. This is also the time to apply an all-purpose fertilizer. During the hot summer months, lawns may be susceptible to fungal disease. It is advisable to take a sod sample to a local landscape expert for testing and treating the yard, if necessary.

In the autumn, lawns can be mowed at a lower height, and thatch buildup that occurs in warm season grasses should be removed, although lawn experts are divided in their opinions on this. This is also a good time to add a sandy loam and apply a fertilizer containing some type of wetting agent. Cool season lawns can be planted in autumn if there is adequate rainfall.

Lawn care in the winter is minimal, requiring only light feedings of organic material, such as green-waste compost, and minerals to encourage earthworms and beneficial microbes.

Maintaining high visibility lawns may require special maintenance procedures:

- Mowing regularly with a sharp blade at an even height.
- Not mowing when the lawn is wet.
- Removing no more than 30 per cent to 40 per cent of the plant tissue.
- Alternating the direction of cut from the previous mowing.
- Scarifying and raking, to remove dead grass and prevent tufting.
- Rolling, (to encourage tillering (branching of grass plants) and to level the ground).
- Top dressing with sand, soil or other material.
- Spiking or aeration (to relieve compaction of the soil).

Environmental Concerns

Concerns, criticisms, and ordinances regarding lawns come from the environmental consequences.

Most lawns are composed of a monoculture (single species) of plants, which reduces biodiversity, especially when the lawn covers a large area. They usually are composed of introduced species not native to the area, which can further decrease a locale's biodiversity and vital habitats supporting an ecosystem.

Lawn maintenance often uses inorganic fertilizers, synthetic pesticides, herbicides, and fungicides, which can harm the environment. The EPA estimates nearly 70 million pounds of active pesticide ingredients are used on suburban lawns each year.

For example, Sweden, Denmark, Norway, Kuwait, and Belize have placed restrictions on the use of the herbicide 2,4-D.

The use of pesticides and fertilizers, requiring fossil fuels for manufacturing, distribution, and application, have been shown to contribute to global warming, whereas sustainable organic techniques have been shown to help reduce global warming.

Water Conservation

Maintaining a green lawn sometimes requires large amounts of water. This was not a problem in temperate England, where the concept of the lawn originated, as natural rainfall was sufficient to maintain a lawn's health. The exportation of the lawn ideal to more arid regions of the world, however, such as the U.S. Southwest and Australia, has crimped already scarce water resources in such areas, requiring larger, more environmentally-invasive water supply systems. Grass typically goes dormant during cold, winter months, and turns brown during hot, dry summer months, thereby reducing its demand for water. Many property owners consider this 'dead' appearance unacceptable, and therefore increase watering during the summer months. Grass can also recover quite well from a drought.

In the United States, 50 to 70 per cent of residential water is used for landscaping, most of it to water lawns. A 2005 NASA study found over 30 million acres of irrigated lawn in the US (128,000 km^2 or 12,800,000 hectares), three times the area of irrigated corn.

"That means about 200 gallons of fresh, usually drinking-quality water per person per day would be required to keep up our nation's lawn surface area".

In the United States, lawn heights are generally maintained by gasoline-powered lawnmowers, which contribute to urban smog during the summer months. The EPA found, in some urban areas, up to 5 per cent of smog was due to small gasoline engines made before 1997, such as are typically used on lawnmowers. Since 1997, the EPA has mandated emissions controls on newer engines in an effort to reduce smog.

A 2010 study seemed to show lawn care inputs were balanced by the carbon sequestration benefits of lawns, and they may not be cotributors to anthropogenic global warming.

With the use of ecological techniques including organic lawn management, the impact of lawns can be reduced. Such methods include the use of native grasses, sedges, and low herbs; higher mowing techniques; low volume irrigation, 'grasscycling' grass clippings in place; an integrated pest management programme; exclusive organic fertilizer and compost use; and including a variety of trees, shrubs, perennials, and other plants surrounding the lawn. A positive benefit of a healthy lawn is it filters contaminants and prevents runoff and erosion of bare soil.

In addition to the environmental criticisms, some gardeners question the aesthetic value of lawns, especially in climates and cultures different from the lawn's homeland in England.

CHAPTER – 15

Erosion Control by Grass

Erosion control is needed now more than ever with increased land clearing not for farms but homes, shopping centres, roadsides, landfill, reclamations sites of all kinds. Almost any plant can be used for erosion control; the most prevalent problem is choosing a coverage that grows fast and is adaptable to the area.

Annual rye, brown top millet, redtop, and many types of sorghums are just a few of the many types used in our country to fill in areas because of the early and fast rate of growth. Annuals are usually best suited to immediate coverage and will hold the soil while plans for a more permanent setting is made. Annuals grow one season and die back, usually never to return.

Permanent grasses or turf vegetation is also supplemented with the addition of the annuals while they are getting started. For instance brown top millet is usually cheap, and seeds easily... thus it is used on many roadsides, reclamations sites and pastures while the Bermuda, Bahia, or other permanent growth grass is germinating. Annual rye is an excellent choice for all lawn and pasture erosion substitute control. Any seed that germinates quickly and produces fast thick coverage is the goal in erosion control.

Bahiagrass is easy to start and has low fertilization requirements but needs to be mown along roadsides. Bahiagrass can be left growing freely on land fields and areas that may not be easily accessible to mowing. It is also used in the pine tree industry and helps crowd out weeds and provide soil stabilization along with habitat for animals. Bermuda is another easy to establish, fast growing Southern grass that has low fertility requirements. St. Augustine is native to the coasts of many beaches and the coarser, older wild versions are the ones to use for reclamation areas.

Weeds

Many grasses and groundcovers that are considered weeds or wanted plants in some situations can be used for stabilization and reclamation purposes. Examples are Johnsongrass, Crabgrass, kudzu, common Bahia, etc.

Bluegrasses from the species of Canada and rough bluegrasses are used in areas of lower maintenance and erosion control. The Canada specie variety is especially adaptable in sights not easily maintained being lower growing and with the tenacity to grow in soils of lower fertility makes this grass ideal for rocky slopes, banks, and conservation areas. Liked by wildlife as well as a groundcover.

Dichondra is a weed in some places but has great use as a reclamation cover and doesn't have to be mown and has a lawn like appearance along with the ability to with stand some traffic. Buy Dichondra Seed.

Buffalo grass is a predominant Native grass coverage that is planted in the mid west for its ability to withstand drought and colder weather conditions and has a beautiful growth and has held the plains intact for centuries. It is easy to plant from seed and the denseness of growth really holds the soil in place. It grows from Canada to Mexico across the mid US Sown at ½ to ½. Buffalo grass has gained popularity in recent years for use in lawn areas.

Blue Grama is another native Plains grass and is used in the arid, alkaline soils and can take the temperatures down to – 40 but is considered to be a warm season grass. It can be planted by seed and has a beautiful teal color with fine texture. This is a slow growing grass and can be mown or left natural. It is found from mid Canada to the mid American states. 1-3 lb. seed per 1000 sq ft germinates in 30 days seed.

American Beachgrass is a native grass in the areas of the mid to upper coasts of the Pacific and the Atlantic and is chiefly responsible for holding the sand dunes in place. It has great tenacity and can withstand winds and changing temperatures and establishes a deep and widespread root growth. Without a planting of this nature the dune area would be completely eroded. These grasses provide shelter for wildlife that lives on the brink of the ocean waters. During storms and in places in places where stabilization is needed this is the first line of defence.

Blue stem grasses are native to the Great Plains and they are found in one variety or another in approximately one third of the US interior and on the lower part of Lake Michigan as far east as Indiana, through Illinois, Minn., Montana into Canada and south through Wyoming, Colorado, New Mexico, and into the south of part of Arizona.

Cymbopogon

Cymbopogon (lemongrass) is a genus of about 55 species of grasses, (of which the type species is *Cymbopogon citratus*) native to warm temperate and tropical regions of the Old World and Oceania. It is a tall perennial grass. Common names include lemon grass, lemongrass, barbed wire grass, silky heads, citronella grass,cha de Dartigalongue, fever grass, Hierba Luisa or Gavati Chaha amongst many others.

Lemongrass is native to the Philippines. It is widely used as a herb in Asian cuisine. It has a citrus flavour and can be dried and powdered, or used fresh.

Lemongrass is commonly used in teas, soups, and curries. It is also suitable for poultry, fish, beef, and seafood. It is often used as a tea in African countries such as Togo and the Democratic Republic of the Congo and Latin American countries such as Mexico.

Lemongrass oil is used as a pesticide and a preservative. Research shows that lemongrass oil has anti-fungal properties.

Citronella Grass (*Cymbopogon nardus* and *Cymbopogon winterianus*) is similar to the species above but grows to 2 m and has red base stems. These species are used for the production of citronella oil, which is used in soaps, as an insect repellent in insect sprays and candles, and also in aromatherapy, which is famous in Bintan Island, Indonesia. The principal chemical constituents of citronella, geraniol and citronellol, are antiseptics, hence their use in household disinfectants and soaps. Besides oil production, citronella grass is also used for culinary purposes, in tea and as a flavouring.

Lemon Grass Oil, used as a pesticide and preservative, is put on the ancient palm-leaf manuscripts found in India as a preservative. It is used at the Oriental Research Institute Mysore, the French Institute of Pondicherry, the Association for the Preservation of the Saint Thomas Christian Heritage in Kerala and many other manuscript collections in India. The lemon grass oil also injects natural fluidity into the brittle palm leaves and the hydrophobic nature of the oil keeps the manuscripts dry so that the text is not lost to decay due to humidity.

East-Indian Lemon Grass (*Cymbopogon flexuosus*), also called Cochin Grass or Malabar Grass (Malayalam: (inchippullu), is native to Cambodia, India, Sri Lanka, Burma,and Thailand while the West-Indian lemon grass (*Cymbopogon citratus*), also known as serai in Malay, is assumed to have its origins in Malaysia. Indonesian people used to called it *serai* too or *sereh*. While both can be used interchangeably, *C. citratus* is more suited for cooking. In India *C. citratus* is used both as a medical herb and in perfumes. *Cymbopogon citratus* is consumed as a tea for anxiety in Brazilian folk medicine, but a study in humans found no effect. The tea caused a recurrence of contact dermatitis in one case.

Lemon grass is also known as *Gavati Chaha* in the Marathi language (Gavat=grass; Chaha=tea), and is used as an addition to tea, and in preparations like 'kadha,' which is a traditional herbal 'soup' used against coughs, colds, etc. It has medicinal properties and is used extensively in Ayurvedic medicine. It is supposed to help with relieving cough and nasal congestion. In Kerala, lemon grass is steeped as an herbal tea called 'Chukku Kaapi', literally 'dried ginger coffee'.

Anti-cancer Properties

In 2006, a research team from the Ben Gurion University in Israel found that lemon grass (*Cymbopogon citratus*) caused apoptosis (programmed cell death) in cancer cells. Through in vitro studies, the researchers examined the effect of citral, a molecule found in lemon grass, on both normal and cancerous cells. Using concentrations of citral equivalent to the quantity in a cup of tea (one gram of lemon grass in hot water), the researchers observed that citral induces programmed cell death in the cancerous cells, while the normal cells were left unharmed.

Tussock

Tussock grasses or bunch grasses are found as native plants in natural ecosystems, as forage in pastures, and as ornamental grasses in gardens. Flint Tussock and bunch grasses, in the Poaceae family, are grasses that usually grow as singular plants in clumps, tufts, or bunches, rather than forming a sod or lawn, in meadows, grasslands, and prairies. As perennial plants usually, they live more than one season.

Many species have long roots that may reach 2-metre (6.6 ft) or more into the soil, which can aid slope stabilization, erosion control, and soil porosity for precipitation absorption.

Also, their roots can reach moisture more deeply than other grasses and annual plants during seasonal or climatic droughts. The plants provide habitat and food for insects (including Lepidoptera), birds, small animals and larger herbivores, and support beneficial soil mycorrhiza. The leaves supply material, such as for basket weaving, for indigenous peoples and contemporary artists.

Tussock and bunch grasses occur in almost any habitat where other grasses are found, including: grasslands, savannas and prairies, wetlands and estuaries, riparian zones, shrublands and scrublands, woodlands and forests, montane and alpine zones, tundra and dunes, and deserts.

Native Lawns

As fresh water supplies diminish and water costs increase, more individuals and businesses are looking for alternatives to water-guzzling turf. *Bouteloua dactyloides* (buffalograss) is an attractive, fine-textured, low-water-use native grass that grows throughout the Great Plains from Minnesota to Montana and south into Mexico. This warm-season perennial establishes itself as a short (three to six inches tall) sod grass and spreads by means of runners called stolons. The runners form a turf that is solid, yet can accommodate wildflowers and native bunch grasses. Buffalograss is exceptionally cold- and drought-tolerant, and has no known disease or insect problems. It is ideal for large landscaped areas such as businesses, parks, and schools.

Although it is adapted to a variety of soils, buffalograss prefers heavier soils, and does not thrive in sandy soil. It is most productive in rich, well-drained clay and loam soil, but also grows well in rocky limestone soil. The one limitation of buffalograss is its intolerance of shade. When actively growing, buffalograss varieties range from green to blue-green in color. Buffalograss will go dormant during the cold temperatures of winter and low rainfall of summer. When dormant, buffalograss turns yellow to golden brown in colour.

Buffalograss is dioecious, which means that male and female reproductive parts are found on separate plants. The female plant blooms low to the ground, probably as an adaptation to protect seeds from being grazed. Flowers on the male plant, often called flags, reach a height of five to six inches and protrude slightly above the foliage.

Ground Preparation

Bed preparation for buffalograss seed and sod differs little from preparation for other lawn grasses. Till the soil no deeper than two inches; rake level, and roll the soil lightly to make the bed firm. Remove all existing weeds. Because tilling often stimulates weed germination, it is advisable to water the bed one to two weeks before planting. This encourages weed germination. Weed seedlings can be killed by hand-pulling, laying a sheet of plastic over the weeds until the sun cooks them out, or by using a post-emergent, non-residual herbicide. You may need to repeat this procedure several times to ensure a clean bed. Starting with a clean bed is much easier than eliminating weeds after planting.

How to Plant Seed

Compared to other turf grass seeds, buffalograss seeds are large. Their large size makes even distribution of seeds relatively easy. Buffalograss seeds are contained within a hard protective coat called a bur. Usually two to three seeds are found within each bur. When purchasing seeds, you should buy double-treated seeds for an increased germination rate during the first year. In double-treatment, seeds are soaked for 24 hours in a 0.5 per cent solution of potassium nitrate (saltpeter), then stored in a moist environment at 41 degrees Fahrenheit for four to six weeks. The seeds then are dried rapidly at temperatures not exceeding 110 degrees Fahrenheit. While the germination rate of non-treated seeds can be as low as 10 per cent, treated seeds often have a germination rate above 70 per cent. Double-treated seeds are stained with a dye (commonly purple, green, or blue) that makes them visible on top of the soil.

Because buffalograss is a warm-season grass, it will not germinate until warm spring days arrive. Sow the seeds after the danger of frost has passed, and the soil temperature is 70 to 80 degrees Fahrenheit. A seeding rate of two to four pounds per 1,000 square feet is recommended. Buffalograss produces runners about four weeks after germination. If cost is not a problem, seed at a higher rate for a thicker lawn more immediately.

Planting can be done by hand-broadcasting or with a garden planter. If you hand-broadcast seeds, be sure to distribute them evenly, then cover the seeds with one-half inch or less of soil or a light layer of compost. This can be accomplished by raking in two different directions in loose topsoil.

The germination and establishment rates of buffalograss are good to fair. However, proper watering can maximize its performance. Water new plantings regularly to assure germination and root establishment. Optimum growing temperatures are 80 to 95 degrees Fahrenheit during the day, and around 68 degrees Fahrenheit at night.

How to Install Sod

Buffalograss sod cultivars give homeowners and landscape professionals another option besides seeding. These sods are produced vegetatively from female plants, and you will not see male flags nor will they produce seeds. Unlike seed, sod may be planted any time of year. The drawback is increased cost. Sod is generally sold by the pallet, which will cover 450 square feet. Some garden centres will sell sod by the piece.

To reduce costs for larger areas, sod can be separated into smaller 'plugs'. The runners will fill in open spaces. Keep in mind, though, that the ground should still be cleared of weeds to reduce their invasions into these open areas. Plugging in combination with seeding is a good way to have a thicker lawn sooner.

In addition, sod must be installed immediately after purchase and needs establishment watering. If possible, roll the sod with a heavy roller for optimum root to soil contact. Initially, water thoroughly once or twice a day depending on temperature and wind. After a week or two, water at least every other day to maintain root zone moisture until the buffalograss has established a sufficient root structure (usually three to four weeks).

Inevitably, buffalograss sod will turn brown and appear dormant right after installation. This temporary condition will pass as the sod becomes established; just be persistent about watering and have a little patience. One month after installing the sod, mow to a height of two inches to encourage runner density and more roots. After the buffalograss is established, water as needed to maintain colour.

Weeds invariably appear after seeding or plugging, and controlling them is one of the most difficult problems in establishing buffalograss. Because weeds grow faster than grass seedlings, you must control them or they will out-compete the grass.

One way to control weeds is to water and mow correctly. While established buffalograss will survive summer droughts without supplemental water, it will go dormant. To keep your buffalograss green during the summer, it must receive 1 to 1.5 inches of water per week. Watered lawns often require more frequent mowing to prevent undesirable weeds and grasses from establishing. Overwatering and watering too early or too late in the season encourages weeds to grow. Many weeds will establish while the grass is dormant if you water too much in the winter.

Established buffalograss lawns should be mowed occasionally, but never shorter than three inches. Mowing at least once a year will ensure a healthier lawn, the best time being late winter before new growth begins. If not mowed periodically, an established lawn will become choked and decline after several years. If you like a clean, uniform look, you may want to mow more often.

Once established, buffalograss is extremely hardy, and can tolerate moderate foot traffic. Neither fertilization nor irrigation is necessary, but minimal application of either at the right time of year can make the grass more lush. A spring application of a slow-release, organic fertilizer with a nitrogen-phosphorus-potassium (NPK) ratio of 3-1-2 produces a thicker turf. Use any fertilizer cautiously, however, because heavy fertilization encourages competitive weeds and Bermuda grass to grow. In addition, over-fertilizing combined with over-watering is a common source of non-point pollution in creeks, streams, and lakes.

CHAPTER – 16

The Importance of Napier Grass

The importance of Napier grass (*Pennisetum purpureum*) can be seen from the role it plays as the major livestock feed in smallholder dairy production systems in Kenya. Because of high population pressure farms are small, with an average holding size of 0.9-2.0 ha (Gitau *et al.*, 1994); sizes are still decreasing. Animals are therefore confined in stalls and fed mainly on Napier grass under zero grazing. In central Kenya over 80 per cent of dairy animals are kept under zero grazing and Napier grass is the main fodder grown by over 70 per cent of smallholder farmers in the region and normally provides over 40 per cent of feed. Napier grass has been the most promising and high yielding fodder giving dry matter yields that surpass most tropical grasses (Humphreys, 1994; Skerman & Riveros, 1990). Reported on-farm dry matter yields from different regions of the country averaged about 16 tonnes/ha/year with little or no fertilizer, while according to Schreuder *et al.* (1993) yields on research stations vary between 10-40 tonnes dry matter per hectare depending on soil fertility, climate and management factors. These yields surpass those of Rhodes grass (*Chloris gayana*) Setaria (*Setaria sphacelata*) and Kikuyu grass (*Pennisetum clandestinum*) which are popular pasture grasses but which yield between 5 to 15 tonnes of DM per year. High DM yields for Napier grass have been recorded elsewhere in the tropics (Ferraris & Sinclair, 1980; Woodard & Prine, 1991); exceptionally high yields up to 85 tonnes DM/ha have been cited when high rates of fertilizers were applied, for example under natural rainfall of 2000 mm per year where 897 kg of N fertilizer were applied per hectare per year and the grass was cut every 90 days the yield was 84, 800 kg DM/year. Dry matter yield alone, however, is of limited value if it is not closely related to the DM intake of the animals. At farm level, the combination of DM yield and observed DM intake can form the basis for estimating the number of livestock that can be supported by available forage. As Napier grass tolerates frequent defoliation, under good weather conditions it can be cut in Kenya every 6-8 weeks giving up to 8 cuts in a year, depending on fertilizer application, rainfall amount and distribution.

It is the main fodder crop in Central Kenya, and is fed to livestock by cut-and-carry; by 1983 approximately 240,000 ha or 4 per cent of the arable land of Kenya was under Napier grass. More was planted as coffee prices fell and farmers took up dairying. About 90 per cent of farmers in Central Kenya grow Napier grass and the proportion may be higher now. In spite of the potential for high yields, actual yields are often much lower and variable and have been measured from 2.2 to 26 tonnes DM/ha/year on farms. This wide range in production is mainly caused by management factors such as the application of manure and/or fertilizer, cutting frequency, weed control, etc.

Napier grass can grow in mixture with legumes. Although in Kenya it is generally grown and managed as a pure stand, it can grow as an intercrop within the same row or within alternate rows with legumes such as *Pueraria phaseoloides, Centrosema pubescens, Neonotonia wightii, Desmodium uncinatum, Desmodium intortum and Stylosanthes guianensis.* When intercropped with herbaceous legumes, cutting or grazing management is adjusted to favour the legumes in order to maintain a satisfactory mixed sward. Napier grass can also be grown as an alley crop with fodder legumes such as leucaena, (*Leucaena leucocephala*), calliandra (*Calliandra calothyrsus*) sesbania (*Sesbania sesban*) and gliricidia (*Gliricidia sepium*). Legumes improve the quality of Napier grass-based feed and also increase the overall yield. Although no longer generally practiced in Kenya, Napier grass can withstand heavy grazing and provide a considerable bulk of feed to livestock, especially if well fertilized and irrigated (Harrison & Snook, 1971) and rotational grazing should not be severe enough to hinder growth. Hay and silage can be made for dry season use. It makes good hay if cut when young but is too coarse if cut late. It is more usually made into silage of high quality without additives. In Taiwan Napier grass is widely used for the production of dehydrated grass pellets used as supplementary stock feed.

Napier grass (*Pennisetum purpureum* Schumach.) is also known as 'elephant grass'. It was named after colonel Napier of Bulawayo in Zimbabwe who early in the last century urged Rhodesia's (now Zimbabwe) Department of Agriculture to explore the possibility of using it for commercial livestock production. Napier grass used to be promoted in Uganda for soil conservation and for mulching coffee. According to Acland (1971) it turned out that very few smallholders mulched their coffee and found it more profitable to sell Napier grass to coffee estates or feed the grass to their livestock. The grass was then promoted as a livestock feed. In recent years the dwarf 'Mott' Napier cultivar has been bred in Gainesville (Florida, USA) with a maximum height of about 1.5m (Hanna & Monson, 1988) and unlike the tall variety, is leafy and non-flowering. Tall varieties resemble sugarcane in habit. Napier grass is propagated vegetatively because seeds have low genetic stability and viability (Humphreys, 1994). Napier grass which is a robust perennial forage with vigorous root system, sometimes stoloniferous with a creeping rhizome is native to eastern and central Africa and has been introduced to most tropical and sub-tropical countries. Its natural habitat is damp grassland, forest margins and riverbeds. Mature plants normally reach up to 4m in height and have up to 20 nodes (Henderson & Preston, 1977). Boonman (1997) found it growing to a height of 10m in riverbeds and recorded a harvest at Kitale of 29 tonnes/ha DM taken in one cut on a very mature stand (more than 2 years overdue). On the tableland at Walkamin Research Station in Queensland Australia, the author observed Napier grass which had grown to a height of over 10m.

For optimal growth, Napier grass requires high and well-distributed rainfall (more than 1000 mm per annum) although it can tolerate a moderate dry season (3-4 months) because of its deep root system. At higher altitudes (above 2100 m), growth is slowed by lower temperatures; optimal temperatures for growth are in the range 25 to 40°C with high rainfall. It ceases to grow when temperatures fall below 10°C and the tall varieties cannot withstand frost, in contrast to the dwarf type which is frost tolerant. However, even though the herbage may be killed by frost, the underground parts remain alive as long as the soil is not frozen. Napier grass can grow in a wide range of soils, performing best in fertile and well drained soils, but cannot tolerate flooding or waterlogging. It establishes well in clay or sandy loam and deep, fertile loam soils produce best growth and yields Napier grass ($2n = 28$) is a robust perennial bunchgrass which can form dense clumps; has large flat leaves that may be 30-90 cm long and up to 3 cm broad. It is a shy breeding grass and seed yields are usually very low — rarely more than 1-2 kg/ha Pure Germinating Seed (PGS) — therefore it is usually established vegetatively from stem cuttings or crown divisions. There are 3,091,410 seeds/kg. It is highly heterozygous giving rise to a very heterogeneous population of seedlings, which are not 'true to type'. Because the seed has low genetic stability and viability (Humphreys, 1994) research efforts to develop seed were shelved and seed is usually not available to farmers. However, seedling progenies offer opportunities for selection and this is how many of the famous Napier grass varieties have emerged. Uganda hairless was developed in Uganda by A.S. Thomas. Cameroon and Gold Coast varieties were developed in South Africa from the seed of West African origin, Clone 13 developed from French Cameroon; Kakamega 1 and Kakamega 2 were developed from ILRIS accessions No. 16791 and 16 respectively that were improved by the author from ILR1 accession/variety 16791 that had originated from Southern Africa. Napier grass can form a hybrid with bulrush millet (*Pennisetum purpureum* (2n=28) x *P. americanum*(2n=14). Bana grass was formerly thought to be a hybrid with (2n=21) but it was later confirmed that it is just a Napier grass cultivar since it has 2n =28. A Pakistani Napier hybrid, sometimes called bajra Napier hybrid is a cross between Napier grass and bulrush millet. A dwarf Napier grass variety 'Mott' was bred at a research station in Gainesville, Florida (Hanna & Monson, 1988). In Kenya breeding of Napier grass was prompted by the rapid spread of diseases among the few productive Napier cultivars available to farmers and by the complaints about the hairiness and sharp leaf edges which easily pierce or cut human skin and makes handling of Napier grass unpleasant in cut-and-carry systems. Some Napier grasses with stem nodes and leaf sheaths covered with stiff easily breaking hairs or bristles are avoided, especially by calves because of eye damage inflicted by the hairs. In Kenya several Napier grass varieties have been collected locally, introduced from other African countries or improved through selection. Varieties have been screened for high dry matter yield, smooth leaves and resistance to diseases. During the selection process varieties were selected that differed in characteristics such as the number of tillers, plant geometry, plant height, hairiness of leaf and stem, flowering and resistance to fungal disease.

Confusion of varietal names is common because no certification system is operational and varieties are hard to recognize especially when plants are young. Several varieties have been in circulation under more than one name even in official demonstration and testing plots unnoticed by those responsible. A key to identification is long overdue. In Kenya many varieties of Napier grass have been collected locally, introduced from other African countries or developed through improvement and selection breeding programmes. The author has assembled over fifty different Napier grass cultivars which are being evaluated and characterized morphologically and agronomically at various agro-ecological zones in Kenya with the intention of developing a key for identifying the various Napier grass varieties using morphological and agronomic characters.

As indicated above varieties include collections from different parts of Kenya, Bana grass, French Cameroon, Clone 13, Uganda hairless, Pakistani Napier hybrid, Gold Coast, at least one variety that originated from Congo, Nigeria, Malawi, Uganda and Tanzania, and some cultivars that were introduced from the International Livestock Research Institute's (ILRI) Napier germplasm collection in Ethiopia through Forage Networks. Bogdan (1977) mentions Capricorn, Cubano, Domira, Ghana, Gold Coast, Merker, Merkeron, Mineiro, Napier, Pungwe, Uganda, and Urukwanu as noteworthy cultivars.

Farmers need meaningful advice on Napier grass cultivars and a practical field key would be useful for their identification. Morphological and agronomic characteristics cannot be used to distinguish all the accessions, whereas molecular markers have the potential to distinguish between closely related individuals. Studies have shown that molecular markers generated by polymeraze chain reaction (PCR) of randomly amplified DNA (RAPDS) have been extremely useful in differentiating different accessions of Napier grass. In a KARI/DFID/ILRI collaborative trial involving eleven Napier grass accessions using RAPDs, it was found that there was enough genetic variation between the 11 cultivars to allow successful separation of all cultivars using RAPDs. The distinct variability has led to the identification of specific markers for potential varieties. Results of this trial confirm that Kakamega 1 which was developed by the author from ILRI material 16791 that had originated from South Africa was different from its parent material 16791 for the two did not cluster together. This study also showed that the head smut resistant Kakamega 1 and the head smut susceptible clone 13 clustered separately indicating that they are genotypically different. Since clone 13 is resistant to snow mould fungus *Beniowskia sphaeroidea* but susceptible to another fungal disease, *Ustilago kamerunensis* causing Napier head smut, resistance to each disease is specific. This implies that a Napier grass cultivar resistant to one disease may not necessarily be resistant to another disease even of the same genus.

Pests and Diseases of Napier Grass

(a) *Snow mould fungal disease:* In the past Napier grass exhibited few disease and pest incidences of economic importance and therefore few studies addressed pests and diseases. However in the early 1970s a fungus causing white mould attacked the leaves and stems of most Napier grass varieties. The fungus *Beniowskia sphaeroidea* [False mildew *Beniowskia sphaeroidea* (Kalchbr. Cke.) Mason] is a disease of bulrush millet too; it used only to appear at the height of the rains and did little damage for at that season there is plenty of feed and conditions preclude haymaking. Studies in early 1970 focussed on developing a variety resistant to the attack. Clone 13 developed from French Cameroon was identified as resistant to the snow mould fungal diseases and it was recommended to be grown by farmers whose Napier have been infected with the fungal disease. Fortunately, although the mould affects most other Napier varieties, it does not affect the vigour of the plants and feeding livestock on the diseased leaves has no adverse effect.

(b) *Napier grass head smut in central Kenya:* This was first reported in an unpublished paper by Kung'u and Waller in 1992 in Lari Division of Kiambu District. The causal organism of head smut was identified as *Ustilago kamerunensis* and samples sent to the International Microbiological Institute confirmed the identification. It was thought to be a systemic smut, hence the precocious flowering of the infected Napier grass. The disease changes the morphology of the plant and is characterized by smutted heads. The infected stems harden and shoot to premature flowering, becoming thin and fibrous rather than normal thick and juicy. Emerging plant stems then become smaller and the total dry matter of the affected crop is drastically reduced. After 2-3 cuttings, the entire stool dries. The result is a catastrophic decline in biomass which leads to falling milk production. Some farmers have to sell their dairy cows while others have to graze their dairy cattle on sparse communal pastures along the road side, a practice that exposes them to increased risks from East Coast Fever.

By 1994, the disease was present in Lari, Githunguri, Kikuyu, Gatundu, Kangema and Kandara divisions. Consultations with scientists at the regional Research Centre, Embu, revealed that the problem was present in Nyeri and Kirinyaga, but not in Embu District. It has also been observed in Molo and Londiani, indicating the widespread nature of the problem which is possibly exacerbated by movement of planting material. It now poses a serious threat to the dairy industry in Kiambu, Murang'a and Nyeri districts. There is a possibility that movement of manure could also spread the disease, as well as wind. Environmental factors, such as temperature, decline in soil fertility and acidity, altitude and rainfall could be predisposing factors resulting in the current increased occurrence, or a more virulent race of the pathogen could have caused the explosion. There is need to investigate whether there are any side effects of feeding smutted heads to the animal apart from the fact that disease could be passed on through manure. Improving soil fertility has beneficial effects but does not eliminate the disease. Cutting frequency could have some effect since it is likely that, as with the head smut of sugarcane, infection is at the tiller bud stage. The effects of crop rotation need to be investigated. Farmers uproot diseased plants but the disease continues to spread because it is often present in plants not yet showing any symptoms.

KARI undertook research to identify Napier grass varieties resistant to the disease. A Napier variety known as Kakamega 1, developed by the author, was identified as both high yielding and resistant to head smut. The favourable results obtained in the laboratory were confirmed in farmer's fields. Once word spread other farmers immediately wanted planting material of the new resistant variety; for example, Peter Ndung'u and his fellow farmers from Gatundu division hired a truck and travelled over 100 km to collect Kakamega 1 planting material from the KARI centre at Muguga. Work began immediately to multiply planting material in government institutions and cuttings were distributed to over 10 000 smallholder farmers within the first year. Now, farmers with Napier grass affected by head smut are advised to uproot the diseased Napier grass and plant the resistant Kakamega 1 variety.

Another serious Napier grass disease which has developed in Western Kenya was first reported in Bungoma district bordering Uganda in 1997. Literature shows that a similar stunting disease had been reported in Uganda and the cause of the disease was suspected to be a virus transmitted by insects. It has spread quickly and now covers several districts of Western Kenya causing serious economic loss in the smallholder dairy industry. Most of the Napier grass varieties grown in the area are susceptible to the disease which usually becomes visible in re-growth after cutting or grazing. Affected shoots become pale yellow green in colour and seriously dwarfed. Often the whole stool is affected with complete loss in yield and eventual death. Many smallholders have lost up to 100 per cent of their Napier crop and are forced to de-stock or sell off their entire herd because of lack of feed.

Some farmers suspect that the disease is mechanically spread through harvesting implements, observing that the disease does not spread until after the first cutting. The disease is much more severe and prevalent in poorly managed fields and farmers have noted that in well-weeded and heavily manured fields, disease severity is reduced.

However, weeding and heavy fertilization are only temporary measures for reducing the disease level and a more permanent solution such as resistant varieties is needed. Contrary to farmer opinion that nematodes affecting bananas (especially in Bungoma where the disease was first reported) could be transmitting agents, no nematodes were found on affected plant samples analyzed at the Kenya National Agricultural Research Laboratories in Nairobi. Insects were thought to be the transmitting agents of this disease as the pattern of spread in one field is not regular, as would be expected if the disease was being transmitted mechanically through harvest implements.

Insects, mainly thrips, aphids and leafhopper are found feeding on the whorls (hearts) of young affected plants collected and analyzed at the Entomology Laboratories and thrips have been most suspect because they were common in all areas/samples collected. Napier grass is normally propagated vegetatively and many farmers transfer planting material from one part of a farm to the other or from farmer to farmer, therefore germplasm transfer through planting material is suspected to be the fastest way the disease could be spreading from one region to another and even across borders.

Napier Grass Establishment

Conventionally Napier grass is established in well-prepared land (ploughed and harrowed) from root splits, canes with 3 nodes or from whole canes.

The material is planted 15-20 cm deep with splits planted upright, three node canes planted at an angle of 30-45° while whole canes are buried in the furrow 60-90 cm apart. The root splits and canes are usually spaced 50-60 cm × 50-60 cm, 50-60cm × 90-100 cm or 90-100 cm × 90-100cm depending on the soil moisture of the area; usually the higher the rainfall the closer the spacing. Root splits generally take more labour to prepare (uproot) and to plant but result in quicker establishment and earlier and higher forage yields. Once the crop is well-established the original planting material type generally has little effect on dry matter yield although some varieties such as French Cameroon may establish best from canes (NARS, 1979). Whether root splits or canes are used, they should be sufficiently mature to tiller well and produce tall and high yielding forage plants; canes should be from plants 20-28 weeks old. Napier grass can also be established by the 'Tumbukiza' method where the planting is done in round or rectangular pits 60-90 cm wide and 60-90 cm deep, filled with a mixture of topsoil and manure in the ratio of 1:2.

Napier grass is usually planted as a sole crop; however, it can also be under sown with other crops such as maize or intercropped with forage legumes (Kusewa *et al.,* 1980). When inter-planted with maize, it is planted 12 weeks after sowing maize at a spacing of 75 x 30 cm, as this has been shown to give the best maize yield. However, if the main crop is Napier grass, delayed planting reduces its yield.

When Napier grass and maize are planted at the same time, Napier grass yield is increased, without necessarily reducing maize yields. Experience shows that both Napier grass and maize compete for nutrients and it is only under high nutrient management systems that Napier grass and maize can be successfully grown on the same plots. Herbaceous legumes can give high yield when intercropped with Napier grass; those that are compatible and give high yields include: giant vetch (*Vicia dasycarpa*) at higher elevations; silverleaf desmodium (*Desmodium uncinatum*), greenleaf desmodium *(D. intortum)*, stylo (*Stylosanthes guianensis*) and glycine (*Neonotonia wightii*) in high and medium altitudes; and Archer axillaris (*Macrotyloma axillare*), centro (*Centrosema pubescens)*, siratro (*Macroptilium atropurpureum*), butterfly pea (*Clitoria ternatea*), lablab (*Dolichos lablab*) and stylo in the coastal region. Generally planting Napier grass with herbaceous legumes increases the dry matter yield and crude protein of the forage. The combined dry matter yield is greater than the yield of Napier grass alone.

Initial legume establishment is slow with faster growth later, however, Mwangi and Wambugu (2001) reported poor persistence of legumes such as *Desmodium intortum* because insufficient attention was given to the legume when planning row spacing, planting time etc.

Fodder trees and shrubs provide useful cattle feed for they remain green and of high quality for most of the dry season, producing ample green matter at a time when there is little available and they re-grow at a fast rate complementing Napier grass forage in a cut-and-carry system.

The most useful are those which improve soil fertility by nitrogen fixation, provide high quality mulch and soil erosion control and which do not compete for nutrients and soil moisture with the adjacent Napier grass on the contours, mainly due to their deeper root system. In addition, some fodder trees and shrubs may provide poles and fuel wood. Fodder shrubs can be successfully grown in mixtures with Napier grass with the fodder trees/shrubs in hedges and the Napier grass planted in alleys between them. Napier grass in the alleys can be intercropped with herbaceous legumes such as desmodium or butterfly pea.

Those that have shown promise include: leucaena (*Leucaena leucocephala*), calliandra (*Calliandra calothyrsus*), sesbania (*Sesbania sesban*) and gliricidia (*Gliricidia sepium*). In Kenya, Napier grass has not been found to be suitable for grazing because the preferred varieties show poor persistence under grazing. Also, most dairy farmers in Kenya are smallholders with very small plots of land, which only favour zero grazing. Thus there is little reported work of animal performance on grazed Napier grass. Although the dwarf Napier grass especially bred for grazing purposes has been impressive in south-eastern U.S.A, it has not been adopted by dairy farmers in Kenya due to its relatively low DM yield and high susceptibility to snow mould fugal disease *Beniowskia sphaeroidea* under Kenyan condition. In Brazil, the author noted that the Napier grass variety used there performed well under specific grazing management, but smallholders in Kenya prefer giant Napier grass suitable for cut-and-carry.

Because of its rapid growth and high yields Napier grass requires regular application of nitrogen (N) phosphorus (P) and potassium (K) in the form of fertilizers or farm yard manure (FYM). High yields of Napier are obtained/ maintained with the following rates of application:

- 20 kg/ha/year of P in the form of either single or triple superphosphates (SSP or TSP) at a rate of 100 kg/ha applied twice a year as a ring application around the stools at the beginning of the long and short rainy season on weeded plots.
- 75 kg/ha/ of N usually in the form of Calcium Ammonium Nitrate (CAN) at a rate of 300 kg/ha to be applied in splits after every grass harvest (except the harvest taken during the dry season, because of low soil moisture) or in three equal doses in a year, during the long rains and short rains.
- 25 kg/ha/year of K usually in the form of Muriate of Potash at a rate of 40 kg/ha/year, to be applied in the same way as phosphate.
- Dairy cattle slurry: this is a mixture of cow dung, urine, and feed left over, available from the zero-grazing stable. The rate of application is 5.5 tons of DM/ha/year or 55

tons of liquid slurry. This should be buried between Napier grass rows to avoid loss of nitrogen by volatilization. The slurry is applied after the onset of long and short rainy seasons.

- Leaving crop residues, feed refusals, mulching, old Napier grass leaves, stalks and other weed trash in the field to cover the soil. An even layer of mulch should be applied between grass rows, ideally after every harvest. The advantages of mulching are: to help conserve moisture and nutrients in the soil, to suppress weed growth and to maintain the soil temperatures for optimal microbial activity.

Phosphorus is required at the time of planting to enable Napier grass to develop a strong root system. Later it requires nitrogen for photosynthesis. Application of N, P and FYM increase DM production but the response may depend on environmental conditions during application and on the soil nutrient status; response may be poor at very dry sites and pronounced when the soil nutrient status is low.

The most reliable indicator of fertilizer requirement is through on-site testing: in most Kenyan studies the response to P was more pronounced than to N and in many cases the P&N interaction was significant. N&P responses were found to be greater in ratoons. Old Napier stands generally respond faster to NPK than to FYM. The response of Napier to slurry is better when the slurry is poured into furrows and covered with soil rather than surface application. Fertilizer requirement may also depend on the feeding system: where Napier grass is cut, carried and fed away from the fields, NPK and Mg application may be required, whereas if grazed then normally only N and P are needed.

Napier grass is a heavy feeder and reduces soil nitrate, K, Ca and Mg status through nutrient uptake. The elements may be returned to the soil and taken up by other crops when Napier grass is used as a mulch. Napier grass is a luxury consumer of K, far above animal requirement (0.44%) and well above the critical level.

The improvement of soil fertility as a result of intercropping Napier grass with legumes has been shown in many studies. The best Napier grass-legume intercrop combinations are: Napier grass /*Stylosanthes guianensis* which produced the equivalent of 400 kg/ha/year of N and Napier/Desmodium which produced an equivalent of 465 kg/ha/year of N. It can also be used as a fallow to improve soil structure and fertility in general. The first harvest of Napier grass should be when it attains a height of 1-1.2 meters, which is usually three to four months after planting. At this stage Napier grass has high quality and sufficient dry matter. Thereafter the grass should be harvested at intervals of six to eight weeks, when it attains the same height. To some extent this will depend on the Napier grass variety and its ability to grow, weather conditions, soil fertility, management practices and livestock needs.

If well managed it can be harvested every month in hot and wet environments like those at the coast while during the dry season it may be harvested after 2 months. Although harvesting at longer intervals produces higher dry matter yields and increased crude fibre, the crude proteins, digestibility, leaf-to stem ratios and ash contents will decline. During harvest a stump (stubble height) of 10-15cm is left; this height influences yield quality and life span of the grass.

Herbage yields from Napier grass cut too low or too high leaving no stubble or very long stubble tend to decrease over time and the persistence of the stand is also greatly reduced as this interferes with the growing points and weakens the rooting systems resulting in lower production in subsequent harvests. Leaving appropriate stubble height will provide sufficient carbohydrate reserves for subsequent growth and especially the stubble of the last harvest before the long dry period will encourage fast growth after the onset of rains. Weeding of Napier grass will eliminate re-growth of undesirable plants, remove the dry root bound Napier in order to promote fodder re-growth by increasing soil aeration, and provide soil cover from mulching which will improve water infiltration and decrease evaporation of soil water and loss of nutrients. It should be weeded as early as possible after planting and kept weed free throughout growth; it is suggested hand weeding takes place after every harvest.

Aggressive weeds such as couch grass (*Digitaria* sp.) are best controlled during the dry season and regular weeding helps to ensure that fertilizer applied after harvest will only be utilized by the forage crop. During establishment, a closer spacing will ensure that the Napier grass quickly forms a closed canopy that suppresses weed growth and planting of forage legumes between and/or within Napier rows will also ensure that the forage legumes suppress other unwanted weeds. Lack of adequate and high quality feed is a major constraint to production on smallholder farms, particularly in dry periods. In some eastern and coastal regions of Kenya, the prolonged dry season can last up to 6 months and during that period dairy cattle could be sustained on conserved Napier grass from the high yields produced during the rainy season, when there is often an excess. Attempts have been made to make hay out of Napier grass but the succulent stems limit the rate of drying and with excess drying the stems may become hard and brittle and less palatable to livestock. The alternative is ensiling the surplus since leaving Napier grass to become too mature may compromise the quality.

However, the proportion of farmers ensiling is small. Napier grass can be ensiled but the quality of silage obtained depends on fresh grass quality, the ensiling process and use of additives; successful ensiling to maximize nutrient preservation is achieved by harvesting the crop at the proper age, minimizing the activities of plant enzymes and undesirable epiphytic micro-organisms (naturally present in the forage crop) and encouraging the dominance of lactic acid bacteria. As it has low fermentation sugars, energy sources such as bran and molasses have been found to enhance Napier silage quality showed that bana could be successfully ensiled when 1 m tall (101 days after planting) and cut, wilted, chopped and ensiled with molasses additive at 5 per cent by weight of material (green matter basis) in a trench silo.

The potential DM yield of Napier grass surpasses that of other tropical grasses (Humphreys, 1994; Skerman & Riveros, 1990) which is the reason for its popularity among dairy farmers in Kenya, who need to maximize production per unit area of their land. On farm DM yields of Napier from different regions average about 16 tonnes/ha/year (Wouters, 1987) with little or no fertilizer. In Western Kenya, Mathura *et al.* (1985) reported cumulative dry matter yield of Napier grass of 40 tonnes/ha after 3 cuts in a year with the application of 100kg/ha of NPK (20-20-0) fertilizer. Reported yields within the country vary between 10 to 40 tonnes DM/ha depending on soil fertility, climate and management. High yields are achieved in the hot and humid parts of zones II and III. Those DM yields contrast with those of Rhodes grass (*Chloris gayana*) and Kikuyu grass (*Pennisetum clandestinum*), which are popular, and which yield between 5 to 15 tonnes DM/ha. Comparable Napier grass DM yields have been recorded elsewhere in the tropics (Ferraris & Sinclair, 1980) and exceptionally high DM yields up to 85 tons DM/ha here been cited when high rates of fertilizers were applied to Napier grass. However the DM yield alone may be of limited utility if it is not closely related to DM intake of animals. Such high yields of Napier grass may consist largely of stems, which may be rejected by animals. Although high yields of 50 tonnes/ha of Napier grass were recorded experimentally in Puerto Rico, the yields of digestible dry matter were only just above those of other grasses such as Congo signal (*Brachiaria ruziziensis*) common Guinea grass (*Panicum maximum*) and stargrass (*Cynodon nlemfuensis*). It is best to think in terms of yields of edible leaf and to maximize on leaf production especially in the dry season. At farm level, the combination of DM yield and observed DM intake can form the basis for estimating the number of livestock that could be supported by nutrients from the available forage land. Serra *et al.* (1996) contrasted the mineral composition of Napier grass with the required dietary concentrations for ruminants and concluded that it is likely to be deficient in most of the minerals considered. Inadequate availability of macro elements such as calcium (Ca) phosphorus (P), Sulphur (S), Potassium (K), Sodium (Na), Chlorine (Cl) and Magnesium (Mg) and a range of micro elements may lead to deficiency diseases in ruminants and may limit fibre digestion and microbial protein synthesis (Hanna & Gates, 1990; Durand & Kawashima, 1980).

The availability of P for nucleic-acid formation and S for the synthesis of sulphur amino acids is particularly important. Calcium is closely related to P metabolism. Mineral deficiencies for Ca, P, Co, Mo, Zn and Cu have been reported in some parts of Kenya and this has been attributed to low soil fertility. Dairy cattle should therefore be given a balanced mineral mixture even when being fed on Napier grass.

Chemical composition of the forage is a major determinant in animal production. As Napier grass matures, the leaf to stem ratio declines causing changes in the chemical composition and a concomitant reduction in feed value.

Feed quality may affect voluntary feed intake and animal performance in terms of milk yield or body weight gain. Grass maturity is usually negatively related to CP content and the results summarized by Skerman & Riveros (1990), Woodard & Prine (1991) and Williams & Hanna (1995) confirm this for Napier grass with the rate of decline in CP content more rapid in stems than leaves. The cell wall, composed primarily of the structural carbohydrates cellulose and hemicellulose, is the most important factor affecting forage utilization as it comprises the major fraction of forage DM and its extent of degradation by the microflora has important implications on forage digestibility and intake. The cell wall content in Napier grass increases less prominently with age compared with other tropical grasses such as Kikuyu and Pangola grass and ranges between 650 to 750g/kg DM. Whereas other tropical grasses showed a daily decline of 0.30 to 0.50 units of DM digestibility, Napier grass only declined by 0.20 units per day which was lower than the mean of 0.26 units per day for tropical forages. This makes Napier an attractive feed since it can retain a given level of digestibility for a slightly longer period compared with other tropical grasses.

Researchers reported that OM digestibility of most tropical grasses ranged from 50 to 60 per cent which is consistent with observations by Minson (1990). However in well fertilized fields, Chaparro & Sollenberger (1997) recorded a range of 65 to 79 per cent *in vitro* DM digestibility for dwarf Napier grass so it is important to bear in mind that climate, soil fertility, cutting interval, variety and management practices may have an important influence on chemical composition and digestibility of Napier grass.

At farm level, the CP content does not always satisfy the 60 to 80g/kg DM which is considered the minimum requirement for optimum rumen microbial activity (Minson & Milford, 1976). A study covering all main Napier grass growing areas in Kenya showed that the mean CP level on farms was 76g/kg DM (Wouters, 1987). Results from other parts of the world as summarized by Gohl (1981) and from Kenya as reviewed by Schreuder *et al.* (1993) indicate that the CP values commonly recorded for Napier grass lie between 50 and 90 g/kg DM. Observations from more recent studies are generally in agreement. These results contrast with those for dwarf Napier grass whose CP content has been reported to range between 80 and 150 g/kg under good management and high fertilizer application.

Nutritive value has been defined as the amount of feed ingested and the efficiency with which nutrients are extracted from a given feed. From this perspective, little information is available on the nutritive value of Napier grass as the bulk of the available literature deals with its agronomy. Previous studies on Napier grass in Eastern Africa have concentrated on aspects such as effects of climate, fertilizer and cutting interval on DM yield, and to a lesser extent on leaf stem ratio, proximate composition and *in vitro* digestibility. Similar studies have been reported from other parts of the world. Compared to other well known tropical pasture grasses such as *Digitaria decumbens, Chloris gayana,* Kikuyu grass (*Pennisetum clandestinum*) and *Panicum maximum*, relatively few data are available on the effects of feeding Napier grass on animal performance.

The nutritive value of forage is mainly determined by voluntary intake, crude protein and structural carbohydrates and forage intake is influenced by digestible DM and CP content and the extent of degradation. The structural polysaccharides composed primarily of cellulose and hemicelluloses are primary restrictive determinants of nutrient intake.

The digestibility of forage in the rumen is related to the proportion and extent of lignification. Chemical composition and digestible DM may be poor indicators of the nutritive value of Napier grass because the farmer fails to take into account nutrient availability whilst the latter does not provide the profile of absorbed nutrients.

Therefore, if nutrient value is to be of practical importance, the ultimate measure should be animal performance. It has been well documented that animal performance is closely associated with the capacity of a feed to promote effective microbial fermentation in the rumen and to supply the quantities and balances of nutrients required for different productive status; thus milk yield or weight gain should be closely related to intake, forage composition and digestibility. In ruminants, the use of CP or digestible CP to determine nitrogen value is regarded as inadequate because they ignore the role of rumen microbes, yet in all forage diets, protein quality of each dietary component is important in evaluating response to supplementation. Current protein evaluation systems partition feed nitrogen into the amount degraded in the rumen and that which escapes rumen degradation. The system is based on the concept that the nitrogen (N) requirement of rumen microbes is distinct from the requirements of the host animal, which is met by the protein escaping the rumen along with the microbial protein. Thus, determining rumen degradation of dietary protein and the amount that passes through the rumen and subsequently becomes available for digestion by the host animal is important. This information is lacking for Napier grass and other Kenya forages. Within the smallholder dairy system, the recommended weaning weight for a dairy heifer is 70kg weight with a target of 300kg to be attained by 18 months of age at the first service (MLD, 1991). This recommendation assumes that heifers gain at least 0.5kg/day but in practice less than 0.25kg is observed on small farms and therefore puberty is not achieved until after 24 months. This is attributed to the low quality of Napier grass fed on the farms and the absence of concentrate feeds. The potential of Napier grass for weight gain in cattle has been investigated with or without energy or protein supplements. Results seem to differ widely depending on grass quality, cattle species and the level and the type of supplement used. Friesian heifers gained between 0.13 and 0.8 kg/day when fed on Napier grass varying in maturity from flowering to early vegetative stage (CP 63 to 96 g/kg DM) and achieved a daily DM intake of 2.1 to 3.1 kg per 100kg body weight (Arias, 1980). Dixon (1984) obtained a weight gain of 0.72 +/- 0.21kg/day from Holstein heifers fed 60 to 85 day old Napier grass of unspecified CP content supplement with 0.2, 0.4 and 0.8 per cent molasses on body weight basis. The author noted no significant influence of molasses on weight gain, FE and DM intake. The mean milk yield on small farms in Kenya is less than 2000 kg/cow/year and although it has been established that commercial concentrates could boost milk yield by about 50 per cent their widespread use is limited by the high cost.

Protein-rich forages (PRF), which can be used in combination with Napier grass, are endowed with the important attribute of high protein content, palatability and digestibility relative to grasses. For example while the mean protein content of tropical grass has been reported as 75 g/kg DM, that for tropical forage legumes averaged 170 g/kg DM.

Several species has been documented as useful supplements to Napier grass: Desmodium spp., *Calliandra calothyrsus* and *Leucaena leucocephala*; others include: *Ipomoea batatas* (vines), *Medicago sativa, Musa sapientum* (leaves/stems), *Trifolium semipilosum* and *Canna edulis.* However, few studies have been conducted in which Napier grass is fed to cattle in combination with PRF.

Nevertheless, an ideal forage supplement should increase or at least maintain intake of basal roughage rather than substitute for it. The PRF overcome protein deficiency in tropical grasses, by providing ruminally degradable and by-pass protein. In a study where gliricidia and leucaena were used to supplement two groups of zebu steers (mean body weight 173 and 208 kg) offered napier grass *ad libitum*, significant differences were observed in weight gain and DM intake across similar levels of supplementation.

These considerable differences in response between gliricidia and leucaena suggest that the variations depend partly upon factors intrinsic to the supplement and partly to the quality of grass fed. Studies conducted using sheep and goats have shown that intake, digestion and weight gains improved when energy and protein supplement were included in Napier grass diets.

"Napier grass is much more profitable than growing food crops such as maize or cash crops like coffee. Prior to planting Napier grass in 1997 we used to grow maize on this land and we would harvest about 4-5 bags of 90kg of shelled maize during the main growing season lasting 5-6 months. We also grew a short rains crop and harvested two additional bags. So in the whole year we would harvest six to seven bags of maize which were worth seven thousand Kenya shillings at a rate of one thousand per bag, so this portion of land would produce about seven thousand shillings per year when grown with maize.

This same portion of land is producing much more when planted with Napier grass: we are able to harvest Napier grass every 6-8 weeks during the rainy season which means that in one year we are able to get 6-8 harvests from this plot; as the harvested grass can feed all of our dairy animals for one month and during our highest peak production of milk one animal can produce milk worth three thousand Kenya Shillings per week, then for the one month we feed the animals on this portion of land we are able to receive twelve thousand (12,000/=) Kenya Shillings from that one animal. If we have three animals producing well we are able to get thirty-six thousand Kenya Shillings from milk for that one month in a single harvest of this Napier grass.

Considering the number of harvests we make in a year from this portion of land then if we harvest every third month, we can make a conservative four harvests per year which would earn us over Kshs.100,000 in milk as compared to Kshs. 7,000 for maize. So you can see that we are convinced that Napier grass is much more profitable than planting maize. We also note that apart from getting money from milk, there is additional value from dung and from the calves that are born and raised as heifers and we also get slurry for fertilizing our crops and can make rich compost manure mainly from the dung and the remains of Napier grass and legumes collected from the zero grazing unit.

Napier grass is even much more profitable than coffee which is normally considered as the main cash crop in this region. We used to have 630 trees of coffee but when learned about dairy farming we had to uproot some of them and use the land to grow Napier grass. Previously we had purchased Napier grass on a daily basis to feed our one cow. We then compared the amount of money we used to get from milk from that cow and then deducted the amount of money we used to pay for the Napier grass feed. We realized that the area of Napier grass we used to cut from our neighbour to feed our one dairy cow was equivalent to the area on which we planted ten stems of coffee which produced comparatively less money. So we decided to uproot the coffee stems to plant our own Napier grass and save money on feed; also soon realized that the amount of money we received from coffee was so little and in most cases we received no money because of the lack of a foreign market for coffee. Planting Napier grass is the answer to that problem because there is a high milk demand in this district and in Kenya as a whole. Coffee prices went so low that we would get only as much as Kshs. Fifty (shs.50/=) for every coffee plant picked. When comparing the production of one coffee tree with a stump of Napier grass, we find that on average one stump of Napier grass planted using convectional method when cut and fed to a high yielding dairy cow can produce three bottles of milk per day (a bottle of milk is 0.75litres). Each bottle of milk costs a minimum of ten Kenya shillings (10/=) which means that every stump of Napier grass produces thirty Kenya shillings (30/=); so in a year when this stump is cut about six times, it can produce one hundred and eighty Kenya shillings (180/=) which is much more than the fifty Kenya shillings, we would get from each coffee tree. Besides, the land area occupied by one Napier grass stump at the normal spacing of 1m x 0.5m spacing is much less that the land space occupied by one coffee tree.

On average we harvest about 60 stumps from an area of about 25m^2 for feed for one day for our dairy herd of six mature animals and wo heifers (8 cattle + some goats). On average one stump of Napier grass harvested at the correct height of growth weighs five-kilogram fresh weight; so on average we harvest about 300kg daily fresh weight. We also harvest fodder trees which we add to the Napier grass in the ratio of 1:3 fodder tree to Napier grass *i.e.* we harvest about 100 kg of fodder tree per day. The total fresh weight feed used by our dairy animals is approximately 400kg, which works out to be approximately 55-60kg of fresh material per mature dairy animal per day. The fresh weight could be a bit lower during the dry season and higher during the wet season because of variation in the moisture content of the material. We chop the grass/fodder shrubs mixture using a kerosene driven chaff cutter and this high quality feed is offered to the animals *ad libitum* and in addition the animals may be given some other feeds such as banana psendostems and other farm by-products. The Napier grass and fodder tree mixture is also fed to our dairy goats, which produce about 3-5 litres of milk per day.

Dairy production is much more profitable than food or cash crops in our farm; cash crops like coconuts, cashew nuts, lemons and mango trees take a long time to mature and become productive, but even when they are mature they bear fruits seasonally and what we get annually from them cannot compare with what we get cumulatively from the milk yields. Milk from this one dairy animal has been used to pay school fees for our children through primary and secondary school and college and has also provided cash to purchase our daily needs. Even during the drought period when the crops are barren, we still get some milk from our animals.

CHAPTER – 17

Importance and Functions of Grasslands

Grasslands, mixture of grass, clover and other leguminous species, dicotyledonous, herbs and shrubs, contribute to a high degree to the struggle against erosion and to the regularizing of water regimes, to the purification of fertilizers and pesticides and to biodiversity and they have aesthetic role and recreational function as far as they provide public access that other agricultural uses do not allow. Grassland will continue to be an important form of land use in Europe, but with increased diversity in management objectives and systems used. Besides its role as basic nutrient for herbivores and ruminants, grasslands have opportunities for an adding value by exploiting positive health characteristics in animal products from grassland and through the delivery of environmental benefits. But even for grassland it is very difficult to create a good frame for its different tasks:

1. the provision of forage for livestock;
2. protection and conservation of soil and water resources;
3. furnishing a habitat for wildlife, both flora and fauna; and
4. contribution to the attractiveness of the landscape.

Nevertheless it is the only crop able to fulfil so many tasks and to fit so many requirements. In this article the focus is limited to the grass and clover components of the grasslands.

Since mankind, human activities have been influencing grassland management. The most important one are the breeding activities since the early thirties in the last century. Improvement of yield and quality was not only in favour of agriculture, but also a lot of grass species were bred for amenity purposes, parks and sport fields.

Worldwide, grasslands cover about 3500 million ha, more than the double of arable land. On the European continent it is the opposite: only 230 million ha of grassland for 300 million ha of arable land, although, the 27 EU Member States converted about 4 million ha of grassland to arable land in the last twenty years, mostly to grow maize. Besides their natural aspect, grasslands have a pure agricultural destination as a primary food source for wild herbivores and domesticated ruminants. Actually, grasslands, being a mixture of different grass species, legumes and herbs, act as carbon sinks, erosion preventives, birds directive areas, habitat for small animals, nitrogen fixation source. As such, most grassland is in harmony and in balance with the environment, excepted intensively used ones.

No other crop in the world has such a wide range of applications and utilizations.

Although grasslands are a mixture of grass species, clover species and other leguminous, dicotyledonous, herbs and even shrubs, this chapter focus only in detail to some characteristics of grass and clover species. Besides, there is only interest for improving yield and quality of a small number of grass and clover species.

Different Roles of Grasslands and Grass Species

Grass for Ruminants

In many countries of the world, pastoral rangelands are the primary and only resource on which both wild and domesticated herbivores depend. As the human population has increased, pastures has been converted into cropland, resulting in an overgrazing of the remaining grasslands.

The grassland area decreased in Western Europe with at least 8 million ha since the fifties. In the same period other traditional forage crops, like fodder beets and red clover almost disappeared, while the cultivation of the maize became more popular. Western European dairy farms are nowadays mostly based on the cultivation of two crops: grassland and maize.

Man's understanding of the principles of herbivore nutrition and the laboratory techniques to determine them, together with the plant yield and quality production have advanced significantly and nowadays, in intensive production systems, the dietary requirements are calculated with high precision.

Since II World War, plant breeding, land improvement and the use of fertilisers and pesticides have been applied as means of increasing primary production. In countries where pasture production is highly seasonal, countries with either cold winters or hot dry summers, feeding systems using cereals (especially maize cultivation) and protein-rich supplements (soybean meal), as well as crop by-products (sugar beet pulp, swill) have been developed to meet the nutritional needs of herbivores when there is insufficient grass to graze to meet the animals needs for maintenance, pregnancy and meat and milk production. In countries with plenty of cheap available cereals, pulses and crop by-products, feedlot systems have been developed in which cattle never feel a need to utilise pastoral resources at all. Since the bovine spongiform encephalopathy (BSE) crises an important protein rich by-product, meat and bone meal, is forbidden for incorporation and use in animal feed.

Grasslands and Food Supply

In the EU, there has been a continuous surplus of food products since 1980 and the common agricultural policy

(CAP) has been reviewed and adapted several times. The last reform of 2003 intents:

- to contribute substantially to the stabilisation of the farmers' income and at the same time to the diversification of their farming activities;
- to be a credible answer to the demands of our citizens for healthy food, better quality, and environmentally sound production methods which respect animal welfare principles;
- to help to improve the public image of and support for the common agricultural policy; and
- to send a clear message to our trading partners, including in particular the developing countries.

In relation to plant products, animal products account for a relatively small proportion (< 10%) of food consumed by the human population of the world. However, if the people in the Third World attempt to obtain also 30 per cent of their calories from animal products, like we do, only a population of 2.5 billion people could be sustained. This is because of the low efficiency of conversion plant material into human food by livestock. Despite the relatively low contribution that herbivores make directly to the diet of the human population of the world, herbivores do have the ability to convert sources of protein and energy into food products that would otherwise be unavailable to humans. About a quarter of the total global land resource is represented by pastures suitable for utilisation by herbivores. From the 3500 million ha classified as grasslands, half of his area is indicated as natural grasslands. In the EU 15 we had in the year 2000 about 55 million ha of grasslands.

Since 1990 (the reference year in the Kyoto Protocol) some 3 million hectares of grassland are converted to arable land, especially for maize cultivation (Carlier *et al.*, 2003). The EU enlarged its grassland area with about 20 million ha (+ 36%) and with 45 million ha of arable land (+ 53%), since the new membership of 12 CEEC countries.

Genetic Developments in Grasslands

The development of new varieties, better adapted to biotic and abiotic stress situations (diseases, climate) and the application of new technologies in pasture management with high fertiliser (nitrogen) input has resulted in a substantially increased output in yield and quality. Breeding work resulted in tetraploid varieties with some specific characteristics and interspecific crossing (cisgenese) grass species (*e.g. Festulolium* varieties). The possibilities of the characteristic pathways for C4 *Gramineae* for a more efficient water use, a higher dry matter production per unit of time and area and a higher N efficiency are only exploited in maize cultivation in temperate regions. Nevertheless productions of 10.000 litres of milk or 1000 kg of weight gain per ha of grassland are not exceptional. However, impacts of these technologies also cause problems of excessive manure, of air and water pollution and of perceptions with regard to the reductions in animal welfare. Problems with too high nitrate contents in water sources (> 50 mg/liter), too excessive N, P and K balances on dairy farms and unnatural veterinarian help with 'caesarean section' for high muscled cows at calving, drove dairy farming far away from the original sustainable production system. Moreover, the disappearance of the complex grass-clover-herbs mixtures by converting native grasslands into monocultures of perennial ryegrass results in a deterioration of the biodiversity. Some specific forage crops like red clover, alfalfa, vetches, fodder beets, etc. disappeared on the much specialised dairy farms. Intensively managed grassland for grazing (summer time) and maize for silage (winter feeding) are almost the two only pillars of the modern dairy farming system in the EU. These negative impacts are no longer politically acceptable and statutory regulations (specific EU regulations and directives) are progressively being introduced to control them.

In July 2002 the European Commission recommended guidelines (2003/556/EC) for the development of national strategies and best practices to ensure the coexistence of genetically modified crops with conventional and organic farming. Up to now there seems to be no interest in changing grasses by genetic engineering, may be because of the difficulties with the interspecific crossing possibilities and the permanent character of grass species (the more permanent and persistent the variety, the less renovation is needed).

Grassland Composition

Two types of grass species dominate grasslands at the global scale: C3 and C4 species; depending on the first carbohydrate synthesised during the photosynthesis. In Europe most of the grass species belong to the C3 group. Their optimal temperature for photosynthesis, on average 20°C, is much lower than for C4 grass species (on average 30°C) and they still have photosynthetic activity above 5°C. Therefore C3 grass species are much more adapted to grow and to develop in the colder regions. The most important grass species in natural and renovated grassland in Europe is perennial ryegrass (*Lolium perenne* L.). Other important grass species, especially because of their production and/or quality characteristics are Italian ryegrass (*Lolium multiflorum* Lam.), tall fescue (*Festuca arundinacea* L.), meadow fescue (*Festuca pratensis* Hudson), cocksfoot (*Dactylis glomerata* L.), timothy (*Phleum pratense* L.), rough-stalked meadowgrass (*Poa trivialis* L.), smooth-stalked meadowgrass (*Poa pratensis* L.) and bent (*Agrostis spp*).

Besides dicotyledonous plant species (*Taraxacum officinale, Capsela bursa pastoris*), white clover is normally a big part of the botanical composition, especially in natural grasslands and in renovated grassland depending to the sown grass-clover mixture the grassland management (nitrogen fertilisation, cutting regime, grazing density) and season (white clover develops best in summer, while grass species grow better in springtime). The interest for white clover in grassland is renewed since the last decades for its nitrogen symbiosis capacity, due to the limited nitrogen fertilisation of grassland in EU member states, because of the problems caused by nitrate in the soil (Nitrate Directive 91/676/EEC). A good and stable balance between grasses, clover and dicotyledonous species is difficult to reach and to maintain during the whole grazing season. A lot of research data and an enormous quantity of literature about the role of white clover in grassland are available.

In old permanent pastures in Europe, America and Canada one can find grasses infected with endophytes. The most common endpophyte is (*Acremonium) Neotyphodium coenophialum* L. in ryegrass and festuca grass species. Grasses infected with this endophyte produce more alkaloids, like perloline, loline and lolitrem and show a better resistance against stress (drought and diseases). Publications from American, Canadian and New Zealander authors prove negative animal behaviours (higher temperature, fescued foot, ergotisme) of cattle grazing infected grass, while European researchers never concluded to such negative effects.

The last couple of years there is a lot of interest for the nutritive role of grassland in producing conjugated linoleic acid (CLA) and . fatty acids. Grasses contain linoleic acid and over half of the total fatty acids consist of .-3 linoleic acid C 18 : 3n-3). Substantial bio hydrogenation occurs in the rumen, but some of this linoleic acid is absorbed from the digestive tract and appears in ruminant products. Studies by Dewhurst and King (1998) show substantial differences in contents of .-3 linoleic acids between grass species and cultivars. There is obvious potential to exploit this finding in marketing products from grass-based cattle breeding. More research is needed to establish the factors determining the extent of bio hydrogenation of these fatty acids in the rumen and to develop methods for minimising these changes. Conjugated linoleic acid (CLA) is a potent anti-carcinogen. Linoleic acid has 2 unsaturated positions: position 9 and 11. This unusual structure is associated with remarkable characteristics: the fat and protein metabolism of the body is regulated by an increased muscle formation and a decreased fat content. Milk and meat produced by grazing cattle contain this CLA and have in this respect a much higher nutritive value for mankind.

Grass on Dikes, Verges and Nature Reserves

Grasses are the main plant species in verges along roads, railways and on river dikes. It is difficult to get an idea how many hectares are involved in this type of land cover. Along highways, main and small roads, along railways and rivers, strips of some meters of width all over hundreds of kilometres are overgrown with grass, herbs, shrubs and trees. One may count some 3000 m^2 of verges per running km, giving an enormous capacity for carbon sequestration, mostly for a long period of time. Besides the presence of grass species in fallow terrains are also an enormous carbon sink, although in these sites the situation lasts for a long period so that C balance does not change.

In the frame of the EU Directive 2078/92 "Farming practices compatible with the requirements of protection of the environment and natural resources, as well as maintenance of the countryside and the landscape", the member states may conclude agreements with farmers for sowing grass or another cover crop after a main crop (cereals, maize) to prevent the leaching of nitrates and minerals and to prevent wind and water erosion during winter time. In Flanders, the Government contracted 4.240 farmers with about 50.000 hectares for this arrangement in 2006. Under the same Directive, the authorities can make a long term agreement (5-10 years) with farmers for the management of buffer zones (5 m width) between arable land along small streams or a wood for an increasing biodiversity. In Flanders, it means a total area of 1.600 ha under this management system.

In more modern times (1950s) the sugar industry used vetiver grass quite widely as contour conservation hedges and for the stabilization of road sides and embankments. Vetiver once thought to be confined to wetlands thrives over a range of ecological conditions.

In cases, set-aside and riparian buffer zones and woods, concern arable land converted to grassland. But this is only a small fraction of the grassland area lost in Europe during the last decades.

It is clear that these types of grasslands respond very much to the new EU policy for maintaining and enlarging the biodiversity, animal welfare, development of the countryside, etc., directed in the respective regulations and directives.

Grass for Amenity Purposes

There are a lot of small, varying to very large, grass fields without any agricultural function. More and more agricultural land is used for the urbanisation and the construction of public buildings and private houses. Part of it is reserved for parks and lawns. The private garden and especially the 'green grass of home' is in many countries for families the identification of their good feelings. People try to keep their lawn in good condition and even to make it better looking. For private and public organisations parks, sport fields and open areas are mainly composed of different grasses. Mostly specific grass species are bred for these purposes, giving a strong dense green sward, composed of slow growing grasses with good carrying capacity. These grass fields are frequently renovated and the most appropriate species and varieties are used to fit with the requested goal. Besides its amenity role, this type of grassland has almost no other side functions; just its water holding capacity and erosion protection effect are positive factors. For carbon sequestration, development of the biodiversity and improvement of fauna and flora, amenity grass fields seem not be very useful.

In well developed countries, the production of ornamental plants (azaleas roses) is big business, while in other parts of the world drug crops (tobacco, cannabis) are grown. To survive, in Africa and other poor countries, the production of food and feed is the most important. A discussion about the possibility to produce the 5 Fs (food, feed, fibre, fuel and/or fun) is only speculative in rich and well developed areas.

Grass as Energy and Fuel Crop

At the end of 2010 the minimum proportion of bio fuels or other renewable fuels on the market of EU member states must be 5.75 per cent by Directive 2003/30/EC. Research and industry are looking for crop production systems that give biomass productions transferable to bio energy: bio fuels from cell walls.

Poplar, willow, perennial grass species *Miscanthus* and wheat straw, recognized as energy crop for the second generation fuel, are the main sources of biomass relevant to the member states of EU. The currently available biomass for non-food use could be increased by proper selection of the plant species taking in consideration the specificities of particular region. The development of breeding programmes for the energy crops based on the scientific findings of plant system biology will allow economically more efficient plants to be selected. Plant genetic modification of these plants via gene transfer methods, is an option for the development of new forms possessing valuable traits such as resistance to biotic and abiotic stress, lower inputs of fertilizers and higher yield of biomass. Obviously this approach has a future, but presently as a whole, the public opinion especially in some countries of the European Union is not positive towards the GMO's.

Poplar tress are transformed in Plant Genetic Systems (Ghent University, Belgium) with a much better cell wall digestibility (lower lignin content); but the Belgian policy didn't allow to grow them outside up to now. Nevertheless the genetically modified crops for energy purposes will be more easily accepted from all stakeholders than transgenic food crops.

Grass for Carbon Sequestration and for Charcoal

Other specific characteristics give grassland more importance. The capacity to store carbon and to act as a carbon sink, in comparison to arable land, its role in the prevention of erosion, the immobilisation of leaching minerals are interesting additional effects in the frame of a sustainable agriculture and development of the countryside.

Grasslands are able to sequester about the double quantity of C in the soil in comparison to arable land.

In this context is worthwhile to notice that permanent grasslands are sinks for carbon sequestration in comparison to arable land. Although livestock enteric fermentation, manure and the use of inorganic fertilizer account for the major share of agricultural greenhouse gasses (GHG) in most developed countries. In the EU, the contribution of agriculture in the total main GHG, carbon dioxide CO_2 is only about 2 per cent, it accounts for over 50 per cent of total nitrous oxide N_2O and nearly 45 per cent of methane CH_4 emissions. Besides, the global warming potential of CH4 and N_2O are respectively about 20 and 300 times higher than that of CO_2. So some agricultural activities, especially well fertilised grazed grassland and grassland renovation by ploughing the old sward may lead to high GHG emissions and transform grassland from a carbon sink to a carbon source.

In some countries, especially in C&E European countries (Romania, Bulgaria), farmers have the tradition to burn the stubbles after the harvest. Under this uncontrolled burning, black parts of stems remain. Under controlled anaerobe combustion of plants (300 to 600°C, depending of the technology), volatile components (oils) are collected. The remaining ash is called charcoal. This can be used to improve soil characteristics. Depending of composition of the mixture of grass species, herbs and shrubs, the nature of volatile components will change and so also the composition and characteristics of the charcoal.

Grass for Perfumes, Alcohols and Beverages

Well known is the kind of brandy "Zubrowka bison grass wodka" from Poland with a stem of bison grass (sweet grass: *Hierochloe odorata* L.) as a characteristic in the bottle.

Other coumarin rich grass species are used in the same way, like sweet vernal grass (*Anthoxanthum odoratum* L.) used in tobacco and herb pillows.

There are twelve known varieties of vetiver grass; the most important is *Vetiveria zizanioides* Linn. For centuries the oil extract from the roots of *V. zizanioides* has been used in the perfume trade. Indigenous peoples have recognized vetiver for its medicinal uses, for thatching, mulch, and feed, and for soil and moisture conservation. It grows both on highly acidic (< pH 4) and alkaline soils (pH 11). Its roots will grow to depths of 3-4 metres. It is not affected seriously by pests or diseases. Each clump of vetiver is extremely dense, so dense that if con*Fig*.d correctly will act as a near perfect filter. The generic name Vetiver is a Tamil word meaning 'root that is dug up' and zizanioides means 'by the riverside'.

The genus *Cymbopogon* accumulates different kinds of essential oils. The essential oil of *Cymbopogon validus*, which chemical composition is reported by Chagonda *et al.* (2000), has been used as an astringent skin toner and anti-ageing for men and has anti fungal and anti septic properties. The predominant compounds, properties and uses of *Cymbopogon* species are described by Naidoo (2007).

The essential oil of lemon grass *Cymbopogon citratus* (West Indian lemon grass) consists mainly of citral. Further terpenoids in lemon grass oil are nerol, limonene, linalool and ß-caryophyllene. The content of myrcene is low, but still enough to make the oil susceptible to oxidative polymerization.

East Indian lemon grass *Cymbopogon flexuosus* oil consists of alcohols citronellol, geraniol) and aldehydes (geranial, neral, citronellal). This species is dominantly used in the perfume industry as it contains less myrcene and, therefore, has a longer shelf life.

Two further species have considerable relevance for the perfume industry: The so-called palmarosa oil is distilled from Cymbopogon martini (Roxb.) J.F. Watson var. mar tini (native to India, cultivated also in Jawa) and contains mainly geraniol and geranyl acetate. Also worth mentioning is citronella grass (Cymbopogon winterianus Jowitt) which also stems from India, but is today grown throughout the tropics; its main constituents are citronellal, geraniol and citronellol plus minor amounts of geranyl acetate.

EU Policy and Grasslands

The EU policy has always stimulated intensive farming without encouraging employment. For some cops yield per ha doubled since 1960, but in the meantime the number of farmers has decreased drastically to about 2 per cent of the active population. It is difficult to understand the logic that the former CAP favoured the production of one ha of silage corn to one hectare of grassland ten times more aid. The challenges we had in the West to face at the end of II World War, being cut from our traditional wheat sources, located at the other side of the 'Iron Curtain' are disappeared. Between 2004 and 2007, 12 new countries got the EU membership. Most of these countries have a less intensively developed agriculture than the EU 15 with on average about 15 per cent of their people, being active in agriculture. Hopefully the newest CAP vision of the EU, promoting and supporting a less intensive agriculture with a multifunctional task for the farmer will fit with the development of these CEEC countries so that within a decade all members of the CEEC will aim the same goal: a good balance between the social, environmental and economic aspects of agriculture.

The renewed and actualised CAP of the EU (Council Regulation EC No 1782/2003, implemented by the Commission Regulation (EC) No 1973/2004) makes grasslands nowadays more attractive for farmers than before. Article 5.2 of this Council Regulation obligates Member States to ensure all that land which was under permanent pasture at the date provided for the area aid applications for 2003 to be mentioned under permanent pasture. The Member States themselves must introduce their own policy in the development of these GAEC, so that the farmers will receive direct payments in return for their responsibilities towards the protection of the environment, animal health and welfare and public health (so called 'Cross Compliance').

Grassland will continue to be an important form of land use in Europe, but with increased diversity in management objectives and systems used. There are opportunities for adding value by exploiting positive health characteristics in animal products from grassland and through the delivery of environmental benefits. In fact grasslands contribute to a high degree to the struggle against erosion and to the regularisation of water regimes, to the purification of fertilizers and pesticides and to biodiversity. Finally they have an aesthetic role and recreational function as far as they provide public access that other agricultural uses do not allow.

The evolution of policies that seek to enhance the environmental performance of agriculture will present major challenge to farmers, the agro-food industry, trade relations and policy makers. This will involve reconciling the trade-offs between the need to increase agricultural production to provide food and other agricultural products and services at affordable prices, addressing the social concerns of rural communities, while enhancing environmental conditions in agriculture and expanding trade. The European agricultural policy is not simple and needs to accommodate also social and environmental requirements.

References

Carlier L., Van Waes and I. Mestdagh (2003). Management of Agricultural Ecosystems and Carbon Storage Balance. *Bulletin UASVM-CN*, 59: 1-6.

Chagonda, L.S., C. Makanda and J.C. Chalchat (2000). The Essential Oils of Wild and Cultivated Cymbopogon Validus (Staph). *Flavour and Fragrance.* 15(2): 100-104.

Dewhurst, R.J., P.J King (1998). Effects of Extended Wilting, Shading and Chemical Additives on the Fatty Acids in Laboratory Grass Silages. *Grass and Forage Sci.* 53: 219-224.

Council Regulation, (EC) No 1782/2003 Establishing Common Rules for Direct Support Schemes Under the Common Agricultural Policy. *Official Journal of the EU* of 21.10.2003 L 270/1-69.

Commission Regulation, (EC)No 1973/2004 Laying Down Detailed Rules for the Application of Regulation (EC) No 1782/2003. *Official Journal of the EU* of 20.11.2004 L345/1-134.

Directive 2003/30/EC on the Promotion of the Use of Biofuels or Other Renewable Fuel for Transport. *Official Journal of the EU* of 17.5.2003 L123/42-46.

Möller, R., M.Toonen, J.Van Bijlen, E. Salentijn and D. Clayton (2007). Crop Platform for Cell Wall Biorefining: Lignocellulose Feedstocks. *Epobio Project*, Cplpress, Ed. Diana Bowles.

Newman, R. (2003). Miscanthus Practical Aspects of Bio Fuel Development. *ETSU* B/W2/00618/REP URN 03 1568 Crown Copyright 2003.

Naido, N. (2006). The Essential Oil from Cymbopogon Validus. *Ph.D. Thesis*, Department of Biotechnology at the Durban University of Technology, Durban, South Africa.

Puia, I., V. Soran, L.Carlier, I. Rotar and M. Vlahova (2001) In: Agroecologie si Ecodezvoltare. Academicpres Cluj-Napoca. 439-452.

Six, J., S.Ogle, F.Breid, R.Conant, A. Mosier and K. Paustian (2003). The Potential to Mitigate Global Warming with No-tillage Management is only Realised when Practised in the Long Term. *Global Change Biology*. 10: 155-160.

Smith P., D. Powlson, J. U. Smith, P. Falloon and K. Coleman (2000). Meeting Europe's Climate Change Commitments Quantitative Estimates of the Potential Carbon Mitigation by Agriculture. *Global Change*. 6: 525-539.

Ten Berge H., H. Van Der Meer, L. Carlier, T. Baan Hofman and J. Neeteson (2002). Limits to Nitrogen Use in Grassland. *Environmental Pollution*.118: 225-238.

Verbruggen, I. and L. Carlier (1996). Nutrient Balance Sheets in Flanders: A Valuable Parameter for Dairy Farming. Meststoffen. 23-29.

Brandt, R.T. & Klopfenstein, T.J.1986. Evaluation of Alfalfa-corn Cob Associative Action. Comparative Tests of Alfalfa Hay as a Source of Ruminal Degradable Protein. *J. Anim. Sci.* 63: 902-910.

Buxton, D.R. & Mertens, D.R.1995.Quality-related Characteristics of Forages. In: Barnes, R.F., Miller, D.A. & Nelson, C.J. (eds). Forages (Volume III). *The Science of Grassland Agriculture*. Iowa State University Press, Ames, Iowa, USA. pp.83-96.

Chaparro, C. & Sollenberger, L.E.1997. Nutritive Value of Clipped Mott Elephant Grass Herbage. *Agron.J.* 89: 786-793.

Cuhna, P.G. and Silva, D.J.1997. Napier Grass Silage without Concentrate Supplementation as the Only Feed for Beef Cattle in Dry Season.

Devasena, B., Krishna, N., Prasad, J.R. & Reddy, D.V.1993.Chemical Composition and Nutritive Value of Brazilian Napier Grass. *Indian J. Anim. Sci.* 63: 776-777.

D'Mello, J.P.F. & Devedra, C. 1995.Tropical Legumes in Animal Nutrition. CAB International, Wallingford, UK. p. 338.

Dixon, R.M.,1984. Effect of Various Levels of Molasses Supplementation on Intake of Mature *Pennisetum purpureum* Forage by Cattle. *Trop. Anim. Prod.* 9: 30-43.

Durand, M. & Kawashima, R. 1980. Influence of Minerals in Rumen Microbial Digestion. In: Y. Ruckebusche & P. Thivend (eds). *Digestive Physiology and Metabolism in Ruminants.* MPT Press, Lancaster, UK. pp. 375-408.

Ferraris, R. & Sinclair, D.F. 1980. Factors Affecting the Growth of *Pennisetum Purpureum* in the Wet Tropics. II. Uniterrupted Growth. Aust. *J. Agric. Res.* 31: 915-929.

Farrell G. 1998. Towards the Management of *Ustilago Kamerunensis* H. sydow and Sydow, A Smut Pathogen of Napier Grass (*Pennisetum purpureum* Schum.) in Kenya. *Ph.D. Thesis*, University of Greenwich, p. 202.

Flores, J.A., Moore, J.E. & Sollenberger, L.E. 1993. Determinants of Forage Quality in Pensacola Bahia Grass and Mott Elephant Grass. *J. Anim. Sci.* 71: 1606-1614.

Gitau, G.K., McDermott, J.J., Adams, J.E., Lissemore & Walter-Toews,D. 1994. Factors Influencing Calf Growth and Daily Weight Gain on Smallholder Dairy Farms in Kiambu District, Kenya. Prev. *Vet. Med.* 21: 179-190.

Gohl, B., 1981. Tropical Feeds. FAO, Rome. p. 529.

Grant, R.J., Van Soest, P.J., McDowell, R.E. & Perez, C.B. 1974. Intake, Digestibility and Metabolic Loss of Napier Grass by Cattle and Buffaloes when Fed Wilted, Chopped and whole. *J. Anim. Sci.* 39: 423-434.

Hanna, W.W. & Gates, R.N. 1990. Plant Breeding to Improve Forage Utilization. In: Akin, D.E., Ljung, L.G., Wilson, J.R. & Harris, P.J. (Eds). Microbial and Plant Opportunities to Improve Lignocellulose Utilization by Ruminants.Elsevier, Athens. pp. 197-204.

Hanna, W.W. & Monson, W. 1988. Registration of Dwarf Napier Grass Germplasm. *Crop Sci.* 28: 870-871.

Harrison, R.E & Snook, L.C. 1971. The Development of Legume Pastures on Hill Country in the Philippines. Rome, *FAO Mission Report* Misc. No. 17.

Henderson, G.R. & Preston, P.T. 1977. Fodder Farming in Kenya. East African Literature Bureau, Nairobi. pp. 149.

Humphreys, L.R. 1994. Tropical Forages: Their Role in Sustainable Agriculture. Longman, Harlow, UK. p. 414.

Hvelplund, T., 1985. Digestibility of Rumen Microbial Protein and Undegraded Dietary Protein Estimated in the Small Intestine of Sheep and by *in sacco* Procedure. *Acta Agric. Scand.* (Supplement 25: 132-144).

Ibrahim, M.N.M., Tamminga., Tamminga, S. & Zemmelink, G., 1995. Degradation of Tropical Roughages and Concentrate Feeds in the Rumen. Anim. *Feed Sci. Technol.* 54: 81-92.

INRA, 1988. Institut National de la Recherche Agronomique. Ruminant nutrition: Recommended Allowances and Feed Tables. Paris, (France).

Index

J

K

L

M

N

O

P

Q

R

S